S0-AZG-317

The
NARRATIVE
ROAD *to*
RELIGION

Faith-full Stories

The
NARRATIVE
ROAD *to*
RELIGION

JOHN C. HOFFMAN

THE UNITED CHURCH PUBLISHING HOUSE

Copyright © 1994 The United Church Publishing House

All rights reserved. No part of this book may be reproduced, stored in a retrieval system, or transmitted, in any form or by any means electronic, mechanical, or otherwise, without the written permission of The United Church Publishing House.

Canadian Cataloguing in Publication Data

Hoffman, John C. (John Charles), 1931-
    Faith-full stories : the narrative road to religion

Includes bibliographical references.
ISBN 1-55134-008-9

1. Storytelling—Religious aspects. I. Title.
BL313.H64 1994   291.1'3   C94-931515-X

The United Church Publishing House
85 St. Clair Avenue East
Toronto, Ontario
M4T 1M8

Publisher: R.L. Naylor
Editor-in-Chief: Peter Gordon White
Managing Editor: Elizabeth Phinney
Book Design: Graphics and Print Production
Illustrations: Michele Nidenoff
Printed in Canada by: Kromar Printing Ltd.

5 4 3 2 1 94 95 96 97 98

To
Howard and Mabel Hoffman,
parents who gave me
much more than life.

Contents

Preface

For some thirty years, I have been engaged in exploring faith with students in both a Religious Studies department and, more recently, in a theological college. In much of this work, I have taken an apologetic approach (to use the technical term). I begin with common experiences of mankind, rather than from a particular faith position. The shared experience that forms the starting point for this discussion is narrative. We all love to hear and tell stories! But stories do far more than entertain us. They play a powerful role in our lives.

The stories chosen come from a vast array of myths, legends, historical accounts, and ordinary fiction. They are selected, not only from the major world religions, such as Buddhism, Hinduism, Islam, Judaism, and Christianity, but also from the faith of peoples whose beliefs were preserved primarily in oral traditions, such as our own First Nations and many African communities. Moreover, a given story is often recounted in several traditions. Wilfrid Smith cites one example of an ancient Hindu tale, traceable through Buddhist sources to the Manichees of Central Asia, to Islam, and finally to Russian Orthodox literature. Since humanity's religious narratives are found in various versions, I have taken the liberty of retelling them, though always, except for the very last example, I have sought to be faithful to the original story line. Thus no sources are cited for my version. A list of narrative collections is provided, however, for those who would like to read more.

Like any author, I am indebted to persons not cited in the text, including my students at both universities. Dr. Mahesh Mehta and Dr. Dietmar Lage, colleagues in Religious Studies at the University of Windsor, and Dr. Paul Wilson of Emmanuel College, read major portions of this work, offering valuable criticism and useful suggestions. Dr. Peter Gordon White, editor in chief of The United Church Publishing House, cajoled and guided the transformation of a very academic text into a more accessible and entertaining one. Finally, as with my previous books, I must thank my wife, Nettie, who once again assisted in polishing my prose.

John C. Hoffman
Emmanuel College
May 1994

Introduction

*To cross the boundaries of one's own culture without
realizing that another culture may have a radically
different approach to reality is today no longer
admissible.*

Raymond Panikkar,
Myth, Faith and Hermeneutics.

*Passing over [to the standpoint of another culture,
another way of life, another religion] is the spiritual
adventure of our time.*

John S. Dunne,
The Way of All the Earth

In Ireland, they tell a story of the time when the gospel was first
being preached on the Emerald Isle. A young woman asked to
hear the ancient tales of Ireland and the stories of its heroes, such
as Dierdre, Cucullain, and Finn McCuhal. She was told by her
elders, who had become Christians, that she shouldn't ask for
such stories. They were pagan myths about people who had
never existed. They insisted that only the Christian stories were
true, and she should not put her soul in jeopardy by wanting to
hear such heathen nonsense.

About that time they saw a cloud of dust and heard hoof
beats, indicating to those who knew the old stories that Finn
McCuhal and his army, the Fianna, were on the way. From
another direction, they heard singing, as Patrick and his followers approached. The new Christians assured the young woman

that Patrick would put a quick end to Finn and his army.

Patrick and Finn arrived at the same time, and all those gathered were astonished when the monk approached the soldier and invited him to sit under a tree and spin for him the ancient tales of Ireland. So throughout the day, the followers of both Finn and Patrick, the new Christians, and the young woman who first asked to hear them were entranced by Finn's accounts of the old stories. Patrick in turn told the tales of the Bible, and all those gathered were equally enchanted by these stories from another place and time.

That is the reason, the story concludes, that when the people of Ireland gather to this day to hear stories they include those from the Bible alongside the ancient tales of Ireland.

Stories and story-telling have experienced a renaissance in both religious and secular circles during the past two decades. The National Storytelling Festival and its sponsor, The National Association for the Preservation and Perpetuation of Storytelling (NAPPS), have taken a lead in the renewal of this ancient art. I have had the opportunity to tell stories in a variety of settings for over twenty years and have been associated with NAPPS as a story-teller, teacher, and participant since 1979. Since that time, story-telling has even caught on with pastors and religious educators as a means of enlivening preaching and teaching.

John Hoffman has embarked on a voyage of discovery in this volume, *Faith-full Stories*. He invites Christians to follow Jesus outside ourselves, outside of our inherited religious and cultural prejudices. He encourages us to trust our fates to the God who loves and honours each story that moves us closer to that compassion which is the very nature of God. John is that youngster who asked to hear the ancient stories, and following the example of Patrick (and Jesus), he listens carefully and well. You see, he is attempting to re-story our faith.

I first had the pleasure of meeting John in the late spring of 1991, when I was delivering several lectures at Emmanuel College. I knew as soon as I heard him speak that I had found a kindred spirit. His lecture during that last day of my visit to Toronto articulated the power of story to bridge our cultural and religious differences in ways that I had apprehended but for which I had not yet found words.

When I read his *Law, Freedom and Story*, I discovered that he had given thorough and creative thought to the reconciling role that narrative could play in our individual and corporate lives. I have been honoured by the opportunity to read this present work in two of its incarnations and recommend *Faith-full Stories* to anyone who is interested in taking the risky road towards a deeper faith. The path may be a rough one, challenging much that we have been taught and hold dear as Christians. But be assured the road leads to the One who is the source of all wisdom and who is the supreme listener to and teller of faith-full stories.

I will not attempt to summarize John's careful and subtle exploration of narrative in establishing and transforming our personal, cultural, and religious worlds. You will want to read the book and allow it to draw stories that have shaped your life journey from your reservoir of memory. I will simply observe that John's work here, for all its profundity in exploring and expanding both narrative and theological issues, essentially falls into the category of witness.

By consigning *Faith-full Stories* to this mode of expression, I do not mean that the work is simply confessional in a personal sense only. While John makes personal witness to the transforming power of narrative throughout the book, he is careful to stress the limits of such self-defining stories. He never insists that the reader must have experienced the world precisely as he has. In fact, he insists on the importance of stories that disrupt our comfortable personal worlds, and that those are often found in cultures and religions other than those that have formed us.

Other persons with an interest in narrative have focused attention on the role that stories play in forming us as human beings, both culturally and religiously. Twenty years ago, as a graduate student at Northwestern University, I took part in Joseph Campbell's workshops and lectures during his regular visits to Chicago. Years before interest in the stories of the religious traditions of the various cultures with which we share this earth became popular, and decades before Bill Moyers' interviews made him a celebrity, Campbell was collecting, interpreting, and retelling myths from around the world. His life was spent presenting glimpses of the diverse and colourful tapestry that narrative weaves across the entire globe and pointing to those threads that different people and traditions have in common.

The first time I heard Campbell speak, I was enchanted, not so much by his stories on myth as by his respectful retellings of the stories of cultures other than my own. My enchantment with the stories he garnered and his respectful handling of them continues to this day.

I have been fortunate to have observed and from time to time participated in this recent renewal of interest in oral narrative. Most of my early story-telling took place in schools, community centres, civic clubs, and public festivals. None of these had a specifically religious orientation. As time passed, I was invited to tell stories in Jewish as well as Christian gatherings and during those portions of story-telling festivals devoted to sacred stories from many traditions. In the twenty years that I have told stories for groups, I have also served as a pastor, an adjunct professor in seminaries and graduate schools, and as the pro-gramme person in preaching for my denomination. My observations on the role that story-telling plays in the conversation among religious traditions emerge from more than an academic interest in the subject.

In recent years, story-telling has become a lens, providing a fresh look at our faith traditions. Numerous volumes have been written on story's importance in preaching, teaching, counselling, and spirituality. Often these writings have viewed oral narrative as simply a more interesting and accessible means of expressing established theological propositions. In other words, stories provided new costumes for the stock characters of doctrine.

While this is certainly a worthwhile function within a single religious tradition, it has severe limitations that often go unexamined. It assumes that "truth" has already been established in a philosophical or theological scheme and needs only to be made more interesting or colourful. It seems to assume that God has put all the eggs of wisdom into one basket (my religious tradition, of course), and little or no effort is given to learning from others whose views of the sacred are different from our own. When attention is paid to other traditions, it is usually to discredit them or to persuade their adherents that they are misguided and that we have a corner on the truth. This was the attitude of those who refused to tell the ancient tales of Ireland in the story with which I opened this introduction.

There is another approach to stories and their function among the many forms of religious expression that are found across the globe. This approach assumes that story-telling is a voyage of discovery. Rather than being exclusively a means of expressing established truths, stories are a vehicle for pursuing sacred truth, which is inexhaustible and always beyond the clutches of human systems and formulae.

The assumption here is that no one tradition has a corner on the truth and that each religious expression has something of value to contribute to all others. Absolute truth, then, belongs only to that which is absolute (whom Christians call God) and all human wisdom contains a mixture of truth and mystery. The value of stories from this perspective is that they can hold mystery and meaning in tension. Thus, they can point us towards (and, indeed, move us towards) the source of all wisdom. This attitude is exemplified by Patrick's response to Finn in our opening story. While he told the Fianna and their leaders his stories, he invited them to tell their stories as well and listened to them with respect and appreciation.

Can a Christian, then, participate in such a project, considering our loyalty to the God of Israel and Jesus whom we claim was the one chosen by God to embody the divine presence in a unique manner? Many will contend that we cannot. They would claim that if we follow Jesus, we must exclude even the possibility that other religious paths might contain any wisdom whatsoever. Some Christians feel their entire understanding of faith threatened by even listening to the story of another tradition as if it might have something to teach them.

My own understanding as a follower of Jesus is that this attitude that excludes the possibility that God might speak to us through other faiths does more to reveal our fear and arrogance than to demonstrate our faithfulness. It limits God too severely, and while claiming loyalty to Jesus, many refuse to follow the example of his behaviour towards others.

What if following Jesus leads us directly towards other traditions and teaches us how to listen to them with compassion and respect? Is this not what Jesus does when he encounters the Samaritan woman at the traditional site of Jacob's well? (John 4: 4-26). He is breaking all the religious rules by even speaking with a woman, much less a Samaritan. His disciples' shocked response to his friendly conversation with her is evidence that even they did not comprehend what their rabbi was about. He tells her that, even as they speak, it no longer matters which mountain we worship God on because the true followers of God will worship "in spirit and in truth" (4:24).

Perhaps Jesus did not come to simply point to another mountain from which we can claim infallible knowledge (in other words, to found another religion). It seems that Jesus is pointing the Samaritan woman and us as listeners to this story beyond all traditional religious mountain tops and towards God who is "Spirit" and thus beyond all human attempts to capture, limit, and control.

A narrative understanding of God's approach to a reconciliation with the world through the person of Jesus is helpful here (2 Cor. 5:16-21). God chose to intersect with our life stories in a human being. When Jesus says that he is "the way the truth and the life" (John 14:6), he is confirming that God's truth was revealed through the complexities and ambiguities of a life story, rather than a theological tome or a plan of salvation. God's story is revealed through the person and life story of Jesus. Jesus continually chose to break out of the confines of his time, culture, and religious tradition by accepting women as followers, eating with sinners, speaking to (and, perhaps more importantly, listening to) a Samaritan woman, as well as making outcasts the heroes of his stories.

Is God's story as revealed in the life and choices of Jesus seeking to lead us out of the prison of our own age, culture, and religion towards an encounter with others like that of Jesus? If so, we are called to a faith that promises more discomfort and risk than comfort and security, and surely deprives us of the notion that following Jesus simply involves assenting to the "right" theology or religious practice. Jesus' life, understood as a story in which God learns firsthand what it is like to be human, and humans are thrown back on a radical trust in divine grace, beckons us to cross the barriers set up even by the religion that claims him as its founder. We are to trust neither in the rightness of our stance nor in the institutions that claim to represent Jesus. Only the kind of radical trust in God that Jesus' life choices exhibit will empower us to embrace the other in love, leaving behind the fear that such love has driven out (1 John 4:18).

In this narrative understanding of Jesus' life, resurrection seems to be the most appropriate completion of the story. Death is the final barrier. Not only does Jesus approach the fearful boundary with prayer on his lips for his followers; he even prays for those who have nailed him to the cross. He chooses to live out his admonition to his disciples and to us that we should love those whom our circumstances have cast in the role of our enemies and do good to those who choose for whatever reason to hate us (Matt. 5:44; Luke 6:27). His story intersects with ours so that we might face every dividing line drawn by our time, culture, or religion without fear. His example allows us to hear the stories of all people, even our "enemies," listening for both their pain and their wisdom so that we too might go to God with a prayer for them on our lips.

This, I believe, is what Jesus meant when he said that no one comes to know God as *Abba* except by him. I am convinced that Jesus was not proposing a new theological scheme or litmus test but was calling us to the intimacy and trust in God that his own life story demonstrated. In other words, to come to God as *Abba* involved following Jesus' example in our life stories, rather than simply invoking some approved theological formula. A narrative interpretation of the Jesus story, then, is a call to a voyage of discovery based upon a profound and intimate trust in God, whose wisdom, Jesus asserts, is "justified by all her children"

(Matt. 11:19). Could he really have meant *all*?

For example, my gift when it comes to story-telling as witness is that I was born a white, male Protestant and spent my formative years in the south-eastern part of the United States. While my stories will reflect this gift, I must at the very same time acknowledge that these very factors are also my limitation. I need to hear stories from persons whose self- and world-defining stories have a different source. Hearing those other witnesses helps form and transform my spiritual journey.

My second observation regarding *Faith-full Stories* is about spiritual formation in the largest, most inclusive, sense of that term. Spiritual formation is a fashionable concept in certain arenas of the Christian community. John's approach has little to do with fashion and everything to do with substance. Everything in our lives that defines the worlds in which we live is part of our spiritual journey. Many influences that are not considered religious by our culture can either foster or debilitate our spirituality because of the way they enhance or detract from our relationship to that depth dimension of our lives, that is, the sacred.

Since I have been bold enough to speak of narrative as witness and its place in forming and transforming our relationship to the sacred, I will offer a personal witness of my own. I was brought up in small Baptist and Methodist churches in Middle, Tennessee. Though I remained active in the Methodist church throughout my high school years, I had begun to ask some hard questions of my own faith tradition. Why did we speak so much of personal salvation and so little of its implications related to loving God and our neighbour when our neighbour's skin colour or cultural background happened to be different from our own?

Every day on the news I saw the faith of persons being laid

on the line along with lives in the streets of Birmingham, Montgomery, and Selma, Alabama—and in Nashville, Tennessee, not fifty miles from my home. Yet I did not attend school with persons of a different race until 1964, when I began the ninth grade. Prior to that time, African-American students were bussed to separate but unequal schools of their own. When I invited Jesus into my heart and others around me testified that they had as well, why didn't that same Jesus who broke down barriers between persons in his time move us to do the same?

In its relation to the war my country was fighting in Southeast Asia, my home church acted as if the Christian community were simply another arm of the war department, offering prayers for victory for us and destruction for our "enemies." Why wasn't Jesus' telling us to love our enemies and do good to those who hate us as we were leaning on his everlasting arms?

These questions led me to pretty much abandon the Church when I went to college. Except for a radical Presbyterian chaplain and an Episcopal campus minister, who was also a first-rate thinker and very fine poet, I wanted little association with members of the Christian community. Instead, I began to study what in those days we called "non-Christian religions," revealing something of our own self-centredness and arrogance. My teacher was Charles Hambrick, who had come to teach at Vanderbilt with a fresh Ph.D. from the University of Chicago and a number of years experience as a United Methodist missionary in Japan and Okinawa. He opened to me the beauty of Eastern religious traditions, especially Mahayana Buddhism.

I never considered myself a good candidate to become a Buddhist, being a North American and already having developed too much ego for my own (or probably anyone else's) good. Still, my experience in those classes allowed me to glimpse for brief moments the world as it is seen and interpreted from a very different perspective. I began to ask: if there is so much "good stuff" in Mahayana Buddhism, why isn't there "good stuff" in my tradition? This quest drove me back to my Christian roots, where I found that there was lots of "good stuff" in my own tradition. I just had not encountered it, or more honestly, had not been ready to receive it.

Years later, after I had completed seminary education and been ordained in the United Methodist Church, I wrote a dissertation on the use of stories from other cultures and religions in the religious education of adults. I based my writing on the work of a Roman Catholic theologian, John S. Dunne. Dunne had written that the spiritual adventure of our time was to pass over to a religious or cultural tradition other than our own and return to our own tradition enriched by that experience and with a greater sympathetic understanding of the other tradition. I recognized immediately the importance of what he was saying for my life because I had already begun that spiritual adventure in my college days.

John Hoffman is on a similar adventure of faith. He, like Dunne, understands that the vehicle for this spiritual adventure is story. They both wish to re-story our faith knowing full well that the faith-full stories they are called to tell will be disturbing to us. Just remember, though, that the stories of Jesus will disrupt our worlds if we really listen to them and view them in the cultural and religious context of their time and place. So will the stories of other cultures, if we are willing to listen to them, allowing them to become parables for us, opening us to possibilities for faithful living that we have never seen before. After all, the stories of the Bible are, for us, stories of a radically different cultural and religious understanding. In this sense, we pass over to them and come back again to our own time and place whenever we study the Bible.

So fasten your seat-belts and get ready for the ride of your life. Be warned, it is risky, this adventure we've embarked upon. But there is hardly a risk-free way to be faith-full if we are to follow the story-telling Rabbi Jesus across the barriers. Be well assured that nothing, not even death, can put an end to our journey towards the one who loves us and others beyond our frail attempts to put that love into words.

Thank you, John, for including us as your companions on the way.

Michael E. Williams
Trinity Sunday, 1994

Part One: Getting Started

There once was a well-respected and loved teacher named Hufis, a Sufi sheik who could do all sorts of wonderful things. But he began to hear of another sheik, Raaleh, whom travellers from the other side of Persia said could do even more wondrous things. Troubled, he set out to find her, and they met on the shores of the Persian Gulf. As it happened, it was prayer time. So Hufis took his prayer rug and flung it out on the water. Then walking across the water, he said his prayers seated on his prayer rug, floating on the water.

When finished, he turned to Raaleh. "Can you do that?" She took out her prayer rug and threw it into the air. Then, climbing an invisible staircase, she sat down and said her prayers, floating in the air. Upon descending, she called to Hufis: "What you and I have done today, the fishes and birds do everyday. Wouldn't it be more worthwhile if we would learn instead to treat each other as human beings?"

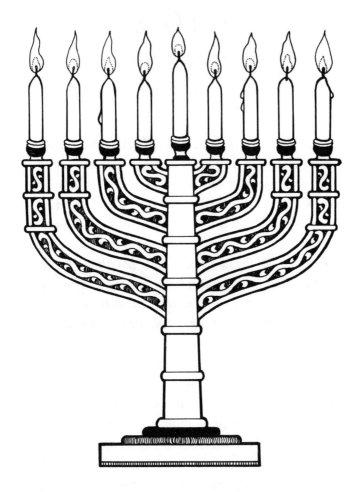

Religions use images to remind the faithful of their stories. For Jews, the Menorah, the nine-branch candelabrum, calls to mind the story of Chanukah or the Feast of Lights.

CHAPTER ONE

Story-tellers, One and All

Anyone can tell stories, and everyone loves telling them, without exception. Of course, some of us are more gifted at spinning tales than others, but all of us easily fall under the spell of a good yarn told by a skilful raconteur.

I once attended a symposium on story-telling. For most of a day, I listened to academic analyses of narrative. All were very scholarly; none very exciting. I had a strong need for coffee. Then a young woman, carrying a tambourine, took the podium and announced that she intended to tell us some stories. First, we must get ready, she said. So she instructed the gathering in a story-teller's ritual. "I am going to tell you a story!" she cried, shaking her tambourine, and the assembled professors cheered. "It's a lie!", she warned, and we all groaned, "but not all of it is a lie." We sighed with relief. Then she began to tell her stories, holding the attention of her fascinated audience for close to an hour. I no longer needed coffee!

I'm sure you've known occasions like that, times when you have really been caught up in a good story, especially one not read but recounted. We can readily imagine some old Bedouin by a campfire telling the story of Raaleh and her magic prayer rug. We need to stay alive to such feelings. We need to keep such narrative experience in mind while entertaining the ideas that unfold in this book. Analysis alone will distort the reality we seek; it will kill the spirit. Admittedly, I shall analyze and put forward my case, but look to your imagination for confirmation.

When we think of being caught up in the hearing and telling of stories, we tend to picture children. However, the potential for such childlike experience, as Eric Berne has drawn to our attention, is innate in everyone.[1] Stories grip us because they evoke the "Child" in us. The story-teller at the symposium clearly brought out the "Child" in her otherwise "Adult" listeners. This calls to mind the New Testament assertion, "Unless you become as little children...." And what are the responses of children enchanted by stories? Are they not wonder, playfulness, fantasy, and the freedom to enter into the story, to participate, to live it?

I have said that everyone tells stories. You may observe, "I know someone who never does." (I suspect that person is often a bore, if not a grouch.) But I press my point: even such folk as these are narrative-bound. All people tell stories. They always have. The absence of written texts in some ancient cultures and among so-called "primitive" peoples in no way disproves my claim. Anthropologists have clearly established the important place of story-tellers, the wise old women and men who recited the great tales of the tribe. Indeed, even among the major literate traditions, the evidence of earlier oral transmission is apparent. Speech came before writing; conversation preceded text. But always there were stories.

Religion and Story-telling

I have just stated that the world of story is the home of the "Child" in us, the domain of wonder and fantasy, of imagination and playful participation. In contrast, when we move to the world of religion, we are apt to see it as a very serious business. Scottish theologian John Baillie puts it starkly: "If a man asks himself 'What things must I rather die than betray?' then he will know what things for him are holy."[2] Sombre words, I agree, but surely religion itself is not sombre and certainly not morose. To celebrate is to say that life is trustworthy, and that, Joseph McLelland assures us, is a deeply religious assertion.[3] Still, being religious is more than casual playfulness. For the believer, it *is* a matter of life and death, the promise of salvation, enlightenment, release. To use Paul Tillich's phrase, it is the focus of one's ultimate concern. Even so, throughout history, religion has been a major context for story-telling, and the spinning of tales, a major vehicle for the celebration and transmission of faith. That we can make such an observation says much about both story-telling and religion.

Naturally, written texts provide our primary data concerning the important role of stories in the life of faith. An examination of the visual arts and ritual, however, further illustrates these findings. When we think about it, that is hardly surprising.

Art and Story-telling. If story really is a crucial element in religion, it must be accessible to believers at all times. But in many cultures, especially before the advent of the printing press and prior to widespread literacy, the written narrative was not commonly available. Thus, in most traditions artistic representations of characters or scenes from the Great Story were produced to help simple folk remember the sacred lore.

The vast majority of Christian churches contain the cross or crucifix, biblical scenes portrayed in frescoes and stained glass windows, and statues and paintings depicting the lives of the saints. Throughout Asia, various representations of the serene and enlightened Buddha, reminders of the central moment in that Great Story, can be seen in most temples. Similarly, Hindu temples contain statues and paintings of the gods, scenes from important Hindu epics and stories told of Lord Krishna.

Here is art for the story's sake. In that sense, we could argue that the removal of statues of the saints or of the Virgin Mary by some sixteenth-century Protestant reformers was an attempt to eliminate what they considered to be misleading additions to the Christian story. They feared lest the mother of Christ supplant her son as the central figure in the Christian's Great Story. They knew how powerful artistic representation could be.

Both Judaism and Islam hold strict injunctions against the making of graven images. Initially this was instituted to curb idolatry, to inhibit attempts to create representations of the deity. In time, however, the portrayal of anything that God had made was forbidden. Though we find a relative dearth of visual imagery within these traditions, artistic expressions occur even here. Synagogues, for instance, contain a nine-branch candelabra as a reminder of the festival of lights or Chanukah, a celebration marking a special moment in the Hebrew story. Muslims also employ visual reminders of their Great Story. Arabic script lends itself to design. A frequently found lace-like pattern is formed from a central verse of the Qur'an that affirms that Allah alone is God, and Mohammed, his prophet. Remembering that the deliverance of the Qur'an to the Prophet is fundamental to the Muslim faith, one may conclude that this intricate design serves as a reminder of the narrative heart of Islam.

Ritual and Story-telling. Religious rituals have an even greater potential to serve as reminders of the faith when they enact portions of the sacred story. To be sure, extensive ceremonialism is not always matched by an equally developed narrative system and, conversely, one may find story but little ritual. With the development of religious life, however, this relationship has become ever stronger. Most important rites now find their meaning in relation to a faith narrative, which, in turn, is kept alive partly through its ceremonial re-enactment.

In Christianity, the most obvious example of this is the Eucharist or Communion, which dramatizes a central chapter in the Christian story. It recalls the Last Supper, a key moment in Holy Week, the meaning of which is enriched by the events of Good Friday and Easter. Whatever additional interpretations may have been added by later theological reflection, fundamentally the Communion service dramatizes that event.

Judaism has annual celebrations marking key moments in the community's history, a history that extends over several centuries.[4] The Festival of Lights or Chanukah falls sometime during the Christian Advent season. It commemorates the re-dedication of the temple following the victory of Jewish patriots, the Maccabees, over the Syrians, in 165 B.C.E.[5] Some debate exists over the details of the story and its commemorative rituals. The Talmud, the traditional, scholarly interpretation of the Torah, tells the story this way. One of the first steps in the re-dedication of the temple was the rekindling of the sacred flame. After the ravages of the Syrian intruders, however, there remained only one small vial of sacred oil still bearing the priestly seal, just enough for a single day. Yet, miraculously, it burned for eight days, allowing time to prepare more sanctified oil. So the joyous celebration includes the lighting of one more candle on the multi-branch stand each evening during Chanukah.

Passover, while not the holiest day in the Jewish year (that is

7

Yom Kippur, the Day of Atonement), nonetheless marks the definitive moment in the Hebrew faith story; namely, the Exodus. It tells of God sparing the Hebrews on that awe-full night when God smote the first-born of the Egyptians. A central feature in the celebration is the Seder, a family meal similar to those marking Passover in biblical times. (The Last Supper in the New Testament story may have been such a meal.) It consists of unleavened bread (the escaping Jews could not wait for yeast to rise), a lamb-bone, symbolizing the Passover sacrifice, and bitter herbs, representing the bitter lot of the Jews as slaves in Egypt. The ceremony includes a ritual where children ask, "Why do we do this?" The answer is the recitation of the sacred story.

The definitive story for Islam recounts God's delivery of the Qur'an to Mohammed. The Prophet is the hero, and understandably, details of his life form important parts of the tradition. Indeed, he becomes a model of Islamic virtue. Muslims, however, also recognize an earlier chapter in the saga of their faith, seeing themselves as the spiritual descendants of an earlier trio. They too regard themselves as children of Abraham, tracing their lineage through Ishmael, Abraham's first-born son. As recounted in Genesis, Sarah demanded that Abraham expel Hagar and her child Ishmael. According to Muslim tradition, however, he accompanied them into the desert to what would ultimately become the site of Mecca. Leaving them there, he returned for a time to his wife Sarah. Later, he rejoined Hagar and Ishmael.

Elements of both Mohammed's and Abraham's stories are dramatized in the *Hajj*, the Great Pilgrimage, a central feature of Muslim devotion and one of the five fundamental duties prescribed for the faithful.[6] Upon entering Mecca, the pilgrims first proceed to walk seven times around the Ka'bah, a large stone structure located at the centre of the Haram Mosque. The Ka'bah is the earthly focal point for Islam, towards which devout Muslims turn when they recite their daily prayers. Tradition records that it was first built by Abraham and Ishmael as a temple to Allah. In an exterior corner is a small, enclosed, black stone, said to be a piece of the original temple built by the Patriarchs.

The Ka'bah is also linked to the story of Mohammed. By his time, it had been filled with countless idols. When the archangel Gabriel delivered the Qur'an to Mohammed (with its message of the one true God), he charged him to cleanse that holy place. Consequently, following the Prophet's triumphant return to Mecca, the idols were destroyed, leaving, to this day, simply a large and empty chamber.

The next major scene in the *Hajj*, the *sa'y*, literally means "the running." According to tradition, Hagar searched frantically for water after Abraham's departure, running between two hills. Miraculously, God allowed a spring to gush forth near the child. In memory of this act of divine mercy, the pilgrims themselves repeat Hagar's search, running between the two hills that are now incorporated into the mosque.

Possibly the central moment of the pilgrimage is the *Wuquf*, where the faithful stand from noon until sunset on the Plain of Arafat, below the Mount of Mercy (some eight miles east of Mecca). Here they recite prayers and listen to religious messages in the place where the Prophet delivered his final sermon.

As they return to Mecca to once more walk around the Ka'bah, ritual recalls another facet of the Abraham story. According to Muslim tradition, God tested Abraham by calling upon him to sacrifice, not Isaac, but Ishmael. Three times Satan tempted Abraham to refuse God's command, and Ishmael to flee, but each time he was driven off by a hail of stones. So the pilgrims throw stones at three different pillars that represent the devil to celebrate the great faith of the Patriarchs.

The ordination ritual as practised by Buddhist monks is yet another re-enactment of a Great Story. The Buddha was born Prince Gautama, son of the chieftain of a small Himalayan tribe. Soothsayers prophesied that he would see four signs of the world's misery, causing him to become an ascetic teacher. His father, determined that this should not happen, endeavoured to shield the young prince from all of life's pain. He was taught the many princely arts, besting others in feats of strength and skill, and won the hand of his bride.

Yet one day, driving in the royal park with his favourite charioteer, Prince Gautama saw an old man and learned that the decline of age awaited all. He later encountered a sick man, covered with boils. Still later, he witnessed a corpse being taken for cremation. Deeply troubled, he was to find hope in a fourth encounter, one with a wandering ascetic whose countenance exhibited peace. The future Buddha resolved to seek such a life. He stole away from the city in the middle of the night, accompanied by his faithful charioteer. Giving his royal garb to his servant and donning the simple robes of a monk, he began his ascetic quest for enlightenment. Thus the Buddha became a monk.

Buddhist males are expected to seek spiritual development by spending a period of their youth as monks. In many countries, the ritual marking a youth's ordination recalls the experience of Prince Gautama. The young boy, dressed in a manner to suggest royal splendour, is carried on a horse or an elephant or even rides in a car, depending on the particular social setting. In each case the conveyance is symbolically decorated to simulate princely status. He is surrounded by followers. At the end of this gala march, like the Buddha, he sheds his fancy attire, dons a saffron robe, and, begging bowl in hand, begins his life as a monk.

It is time to shake the tambourine and step into the world of story. "Not all of it is a lie," but much of it is puzzling. We shall ask why stories are so widely used. We shall inquire about the variety of tales told, what they mean, and how they affect us. We shall face perhaps the most troubling question for many: does it make sense to claim they are true? Our challenge will be to combine the intellectual honesty of rational inquiry with the spontaneity and playfulness of our imagination. This creative tension is necessary if we are to enter truly into the world of story and of faith.

Stories, as we shall see, do more than entertain. They are powerful and delicate instruments, shaping our identity, defining our meanings. They are transmuters, carrying us into those mysterious depths of life that we cannot master but where we must learn to cope and, entering into them, be transformed.

> *When misfortune threatened the Jews, the great Rabbi Israel Baal Shem-Tov would go into a certain part of the forest to meditate. There he would light a fire, say a special prayer, and a miracle would happen to avert the misfortune.*
>
> *Later, when his famous disciple the Magid of Mezritch feared some disaster and wished to intercede with heaven, he would go to the same place in the forest and say: "Master of the Universe, listen! I have forgotten how to light the fire, but I still remember the prayer," and again a miracle would happen.*
>
> *Still later, Rabbi Moshe-Leib of Sasov, when it was time to save his people, would return to the forest and say: "I do not know how to light the fire, I have forgotten the prayer, but I know the place and this must suffice." It was enough, and a miracle happened yet again.*

Then it fell to Rabbi Israel of Rizhyn to prevent misfortune. Sitting in his armchair, his head in his hands, he talked with God: "I am unable to light the fire and I have forgotten the prayer; I do not even know the way in the forest. All I can do is retell the story. That must be enough." And it was.

God made us because God loves stories.

Part Two:
Why Stories?

Why do people use stories to express their faith? The answer is somewhat more complicated than we might assume. In this section, I will sketch three important answers. The first relates to our individual and communal sense of identity. John Smith and Mary Brown, as well as the communities to which they belong, understand themselves and their world through stories. Moreover, those stories reflect value judgements and fundamental assumptions that give such sense of identity a religious character.

My second and third answers to the Why? question relate to the effect of stories upon us. Narratives, we shall see, in all their richness as playful fantasy and as an invitation to participate, have a powerful affect upon the way we listeners think. At the purely conceptual level, the playful fantasy invoked by stories provides a way to talk about those things (such as God) that transcend all thought. Yet religions are more than systems of ideas or collections of doctrine. All great faith traditions claim to offer believers ultimate transformation. It may be called salvation or release or enlightenment. Here too it is the play of imagination, liberated by stories, that provides a potent means of personal and social transformation. Not surprisingly then, religions have gravitated to stories as the chosen form of expression.

By recounting the great stories of their people, the old men and women in traditional cultures played a crucial role in sustaining them as a community. (Artist's interpretation of a detail from The Last Supper *by Richard West.)*

CHAPTER TWO

To Remind Us Who We Are

The Narrative Nature of Identity

Clearly some aspects of personal identity do not appear story-like. Mary Brown is a forty-five-year-old mother of three. She works as a senior loans officer in a large bank, attends the local Baptist church on occasion, and swims and plays tennis regularly to keep in shape. Much of this is hard data, useful for some purposes, just as weight, height, and blood pressure may be helpful to her doctor. However, we would hardly call this narrative. Such factual descriptions lack the very thing we seek, the human reality. We want to know what kind of mother she is. Does she play with her kids? Help with their homework? Or is she too busy? Where did she get her passion for exercise? We want some sense of her self-image as a single mother and as a bank executive, and what she thinks about on those occasional Sundays in church. All of this, I suggest, is normally conveyed by relating incidents that make her come alive for us.

Sam Keen shares a story, in this case, a memory, to describe his father. He even begins with, "Once upon a time...."[1] He tells of his father's skill in carving little monkeys out of peach seeds. His father had promised to carve one sometime for Sam. Years passed, and the promised monkey never arrived. Shortly before his father's death, Sam confided to him that only once had the older man failed him: he had never carved that monkey. Soon after, Sam received a peach-seed monkey through the mail. Enclosed was a note conceding that the monkey was not perfect. One leg had been broken and repaired with glue. His father apologized, for he lacked sufficient time to carve a perfect one. He died soon after this. These events further shaped Keen's understanding of his father and of his love and fidelity. The monkey became a symbol of promises made and kept, and of his father's care, which had nurtured him.

We do not know when Sam Keen or his father were born. We do not know the height, weight, or occupation of either of them. However, we gain a deeper awareness of Keen and his father as persons than we could ever capture with such objective data. Keen has given us a slice of life, a mini-drama, a moment with his father that makes both men real for us.

In recounting this narrative, Keen has, of course, been selective. He has chosen an event particularly revealing of who his father was or, at least, who he was for Sam Keen. He has been selective, though not dishonest. All history is selective. Scholars cannot begin to record every fact, person, or attitude. They must choose those they judge as crucial to an understanding of the event, era, or personality discussed. They do not tell us what Napoleon ate for breakfast before the Battle of Waterloo, or the colour of Anne Boleyn's dress on the day of her execution, even if such details are known. They would do so only if they felt these facts were important in understanding Napoleon's defeat or the sad queen's defiance of King Henry.

The teller of history, like the teller of stories, must determine what to recall for us. The narratives and/or histories that convey our deepest sense of persons likewise reflect a series of choices, a selection of those events or behaviour patterns felt most fully to disclose who they are. Identity, whether of an individual or of a community, is conveyed in a story, a selective recounting of history.

A further refinement is brought to our attention by modern psychotherapy. There are two kinds of history. H. Richard Niebuhr calls these external and internal history.[2] External history is history as seen from the outside; for example, the account of the Napoleonic wars as described by a disinterested scholar one hundred years later. Internal history is a recounting of events as experienced by the deeply involved participant who understands him/herself in terms of its crucial events.

Imagine a ten-year-old girl who has lost her sight as the result of a tragic accident. She is sent to a school for the blind, learns Braille, eventually graduates, and goes on to become a physiotherapist. At the age of thirty-five, when she is married, with two children, she hears of an exciting, new surgical technique for treating her type of nerve damage. The surgery is scheduled and is a success. Over a period of six months, she gradually regains her sight.

This account is external history, what one might read in the medical records. Contrast this with the woman's personal experience, with the story she could relate! What was it like for her to be ten years of age and lose her sight? She could tell of the darkness, the fear, the frustration, the painful adjustments. She could speak of her renewed confidence when she entered a profession where blindness was in some ways an asset. What was it like to meet and marry a man whom she recognized only by the sound of his voice, the touch of his hand? What was it like to be a mother who knew her children only by the way they nursed at her breast or tugged at her skirt? What was it like to have the light return, to see the family she loved for the first time? That account would be internal history, truly her-story!

Psychotherapists from many schools have argued that we all live and understand ourselves in terms of such tales, although they are less dramatic for most of us. Alfred Adler wrote that

> *the greatest of all helps, however, in gaining a quick comprehension of the meaning an individual gives to himself and to life comes through his memories. Every memory, however trivial he may think it, represents to him something* memorable. *It is memorable because of its bearing on life as he pictures it.*[3]

Adler found that, whether as a result of therapy or simply of new life experiences, significant changes in one's self-understanding are always accompanied by a shift in the memories that sustain that understanding. Moreover, it is irrelevant whether or not these memories are accurate. The key point is that they represent what the individual believes.[4]

Furthermore, narratives can powerfully shape our dreams, our heroes, and our sense of self, even when clearly recognized as fictional accounts. The heroes and villains of television dramas shape, sometimes tragically, the lives of many viewers.

W. C. Smith provides an interesting example of this. In the story of Barlaam and Josaphat, a tale which had a profound affect on Russian thought and literature, Tolstoy encountered a fable that had a great influence on him. The fable in question likens the human condition to a man who, fleeing a savage beast, falls into a deep well in which there is a devouring dragon. The man is saved, temporarily, by clinging to a bush. Its roots, however, are slowly being eaten away by two mice. From the bush drops honey, which at first is sweet but soon loses it savour. Such is our earthly condition. We know that one day we must lose all and die.

The impact of this tale was dramatic, according to Smith. Tolstoy traded his wealthy, materialistic lifestyle for a deeply religious and ascetic one. He said of the story, "This is no fable. It is real unanswerable truth."[5] In our discussion of religious narratives, we shall discover that whole faith communities have freely invoked such tales to convey their view of nature, humanity, and God.

Narrative is an important vehicle, not only for individuals, but also for collective self-understanding. The group may be small, perhaps only a family. Elizabeth Stone, professor of English and Media Studies, has recorded the wide variety of "family stories" that shaped those she interviewed from many walks of life.[6] The community can, of course, be as large as an entire nation. What does it mean, in a truly personal sense, to be English, German, Russian, Chinese, Canadian, or American? Surely it is more than the objective data that one was born in the city of Liverpool, Hamburg, Kiev, Beijing, Winnipeg, or Boston. It is even more than a common external history. It includes sharing heroes and symbols, and claiming certain events. To be English, for instance, is to have images of Nelson, Florence Nightingale, Queen Elizabeth I, and Winston Churchill. It is to remember playing darts at the local pub, thumbing one's nose at Hitler and the Luftwaffe during the Battle of Britain, and knowing the Fab Four came from Liverpool. The older the nation, the more numerous the tales that define the citizen.

In *The Meaning of Revelation*, H. Richard Niebuhr compares two accounts of 1776. The *Cambridge Modern History* records the external history.

On July 4, 1776, Congress passed the resolution which made the colonies independent communities, issuing at the same time the well known Declaration of Independence. If we regard the Declaration as the assertion of an abstract political theory, criticism and condemnation are easy. It sets out with a general proposition so vague as to be practically useless. The doctrine of the equality of men, unless it be qualified and conditioned by reference to special circumstances, is either a barren truth or a delusion.

As an American, Lincoln offers internal history.

Four score and seven years ago our fathers *brought forth upon this continent a new nation, conceived in liberty and dedicated to the proposition that all men are created equal.*[7]

Let me propose a third account of 1776 that might be told by our First Nations as part of their internal history.

In the seventeenth century, our ancestors held a naive immigration policy that welcomed all, including strange, white-skinned people. They helped the newcomers through the first hard winters, but gradually these strangers began to claim all the land, the land given to our fathers and mothers by the Great Spirit, the land where they now sleep in their graves. All, they said, was theirs by right of discovery and conquest. Had we not discovered it long before? Had we not welcomed them as friends? Then they fought among themselves in 1776 and called it a "war of

independence," declaring all to be equal, all, it seems,
except us.

What about religious identity? What does it mean to be
Jewish, Muslim, Jain, or Hindu? The external observer might
note that Jews do not eat pork. They worship in buildings called
synagogues. Jerusalem is their holy city, and they model their
lives (ideally at least) on the law of God given through Moses.
But what does it mean to a Jew to be Jewish, to a Muslim or a
Hindu to be a believer? It means sharing an internal history of
how it all began and living with stories of heroes and hopes of
how it will all end.

Consider Israelite identity. Viewed externally, the second
millennium B.C.E. was marked by waves of migrations as the
result of social, political, and economic forces. Clusters of people
appear to have moved out of the Tigris and Euphrates valleys,
across the fertile Crescent, which includes present-day Syria
and Iraq, down into Palestine. Among these were the forebears
of the Israelites. Still later, the external observer would note a
loosely knit community of slaves escaping from Egypt and a
people, the Habiru, appearing in Canaan.

For the Israelites, however, all this was the story of Yahweh's
dealings with a chosen people. God called Abraham to leave Ur
of the Chaldees. God arranged Joseph's appointment as chief
advisor to Pharaoh. God heard the cry of the Hebrew slaves and
sent Moses as the agent of their deliverance. Much of this was
recalled liturgically in a ceremony taking place centuries after
the Exodus event. When people brought their offering to the
temple they would recite these words:

A wandering Aramean was my ancestor; he went
down into Egypt and lived there as an alien, few in

number, and there he became a great nation, mighty and populous. When the Egyptians treated us harshly and afflicted us, by imposing hard labor on us, we cried to the Lord, the God of our ancestors; the Lord heard our voice and saw our affliction, our toil, and our oppression. The Lord brought us out of Egypt with a mighty hand and an outstretched arm, with a terrifying display of power, and with signs and wonders; and he brought us into this place and gave us this land, a land flowing with milk and honey. So now I bring the first of the fruit of the ground that you, O Lord, have given me.

(Deut. 26:5-10, NRSV; emphasis mine)

(The pronouns make clear the profoundly self-defining character of this history.)

The Story Is Always Religious

Religious identity, then, like any other, is expressed in terms of self- and world-defining stories. Even so, merely to note that tells us something about identity in general but little about its relationship to religion. More must be said.

The writing of self-, community-, and world-defining stories reflects a history of value-laden decisions. Let us unpack this important statement.

What does it mean to be a man or a woman, to be a mechanic, a nurse, a lawyer, an office worker, a student? What does it mean to be pregnant, unemployed, or of a "different" race? What does it mean to be a success or a failure? In large measure, for the individual, it means essentially whatever society says it means.

We are profoundly shaped by cultural definitions.[8]

When he was five, my son cut his hand and required stitches. At the hospital he was given a big sucker as a reward for bravery, but since it was close to supper, his mother put it away. After the meal, as a typically proud father, I made a big deal of it, pinning the sucker on his shirt as the *Croix de Guerre*. When I tried, however, to kiss him on both cheeks with true Gallic flair, he jumped back. "Daddy, soldiers don't kiss!" Clearly he had a firm image of what it meant to be a soldier. Where did he get it? Surely he absorbed it from our culture, probably through television.

Similarly, what it means to the individual to be young, single, and pregnant, to be unemployed, to be black, is shaped significantly by the way one's community understands and reacts to such persons. We choose from among the options presented by society. Nevertheless, while these "scripts" are essentially written by society, there remains significant freedom in choosing which roles to play and how to play them.

Most societies are complex, embracing a variety of subcultures, but not all groups exercise the same influence. Sociologists speak of this in terms of one's *significant other(s)*. As might be expected, those communities with which we are in direct contact normally play the most important role. Individuals, however, may reject or significantly modify the definitions of the dominant culture out of allegiance to a subgroup within society whose values are preferred. They may do so even when that society exercises the power to enforce its will through punishment and death. A person of exceptional inner strength may hold firm to the definitions of a community with which there is no direct contact, even a community which at that moment does not actually exist. It could be argued that the great religious founders and reformers were persons of precisely that character. In religious terms, they chose to obey God rather than men. In sociological terms, they chose to identify with ideal social definitions whose legitimation lay solely in their moral authority.

The story of Celie in Alice Walker's *The Color Purple* reflects both the power of the dominant society and the freedom to create a new self. She becomes a new woman when she chooses to identify with a preferred subculture and adopts new heroes. The socially accepted role of a Black woman and the life which Celie experiences calls for submission to the sexual desires of men and for doing most of the work. Moreover, she could expect to be beaten regularly in the black community and abused by the white. All around her people live out that script. Indeed, it seems so right that she suggests to her stepson that he should beat his wife if she will not obey. In her own eyes, she is ugly and unloved, at least since her husband drove away her sister, Nettie, the only person ever to love her. Her self-image matches her husband's taunt that she is a poor, ugly, Black woman; in short, worthless.[9]

Into Celie's life come two black women who reject that script. Sofia, strong and self-confident, allows no one to push her around, not even the white mayor. For this she ends up in jail. Not even her husband, Harpo. When he tries to beat her, she thrashes him. Angrily she confronts Celie, who has encouraged him. For all of her life, Sofia has had to fight the men in her family, her father, brothers, uncles, and cousins. God knows she loves Harpo, but she will not let him beat her. She will kill him first.[10]

In addition, Celie discovers Shug Avery, a sexy night club singer who for years has carried on an affair with Celie's husband. She symbolizes beauty in contrast to Celie's ugliness.

With Celie's husband, she is not the beaten and obedient woman, but the one who gives orders. More than this, she shows Celie love. With her, Celie finds the beauty and tenderness of sex, and finds someone who does not treat her as dirt.

Sofia and Shug become Celie's significant others, a new definitive community for Celie, gradually changing her self-image. The day arrives when she calmly announces that she is leaving her husband to create a life of her own, but that one day she and her sister Nettie will come back and whip his ass.[11] She has made her choices; she has a new self-image. And this new identity, like all such, is largely unique to Celie.

Clearly, identity is not something formed and fixed once and for all; it is constantly being re-created. It develops through an ongoing series of decisions concerning oneself and the "important" things. It develops through commitments to accept or reject the roles and definitions offered by others. Individual identity lives in a personal narrative that recalls those moments of choices made, old images altered, and new elements added to one's self-understanding.

In a word, I am convinced that stories are the most effective vehicles for expressing identity. They do so in part by recording, more or less accurately, the history of past choices that have shaped the evolving sense of who one is. This process inevitably implies structuring one's allegiances, ordering one's values, accepting basic assumptions concerning the world and our place in it. Surely this is akin to what is meant by acknowledging a god or gods. Not all decisions, of course, are equally definitive; not all involve that which Paul Tillich calls our "ultimate concern."[12] Still the process of identity formation, I suggest, has basic attributes normally associated with religion.

Story and Revelation

Finally, from this perspective let me say something about that which faith calls revelation. I am not asking the theological question of whether there is a personal god revealing divine truth; I refer only to the human experience to which the term revelation has been applied.

We have seen that persons and groups understand themselves in terms of self-defining stories. Some are actually histories shaped by moments that have a special and definitive meaning for them. Some are pure fiction, which, in similar fashion, come alive with meaning. Here I suggest is the clue to the *human* experience of revelation. It refers to those experiences, those moments that become "chapters" in our personal story, ordering and illuminating that story. For example, whatever the events associated with the departure of a band of slaves from Egypt around 1250 B.C.E., they did not make a major impact on Egyptian history. For the Hebrews, however, they became world-defining! Similarly, stories that we know to be pure fiction may transform us.

Revelatory events need not be spectacular. They may be hearing a powerful tale or a passage of sacred literature. They may take the form of a beautiful or disturbing scene. They need not, from an external perspective, appear as "religious." For the individual or group, the crucial factor is the power of the event to become definitive, to be a significant element in determining how they perceive and respond to reality. Revelation as a purely human category refers to the experience of such self- and world-defining moments.

Gandhi recorded such an event. In his youth, he felt the need to confess an act of petty theft to his father but could not bring himself to speak the words. So he wrote out his confession, handed it to his father, and sat down before him. Tears ran down his father's cheeks as he read the note. In his agony, he silently tore it up. Gandhi could see his father's torment and cried also. "This was, for me an object-lesson in Ahimsa [non-violence]. Then I could read in it nothing more than a father's love, but today I know it was pure Ahimsa."[13]

For Gandhi, that event lived as a definitive memory of his father and the meaning of paternal love. Even more, it became an element in shaping his own lifestyle, one marked by devotion to non-violence. His father did not punish him, nor did he grimace and give way to anger, as so many fathers would have done. Rather, he bore his agony in silence.

Elie Wiesel has played a prominent part in the attempt of the Jewish people to come to terms with the Holocaust. In *Night,* his moving story of the death camps, he vividly portrays how his life was profoundly shaped by those shattering experiences. The work is a litany of the traumatic events that tore apart the simple piety of a devout Jewish boy and left him forever destined to struggle with the mystery of human iniquity. Yet some scenes stand out; some passages speak louder than others.

He describes his first night in camp: little children destined for fiery oblivion, the smoke, the flames that consumed his faith. "Never shall I forget," he wrote, "those moments which murdered my God and my soul and turned my dreams to dust."[14]

Again let me stress that revelatory incidents need not appear dramatic to the external witness. John Wesley felt his heart being strangely warmed at a prayer meeting in Aldersgate. The Buddha came to his experience of enlightenment under the bodhi tree. Tolstoy was profoundly changed upon reading a fable within the story of Barlaam and Josaphat. It is unlikely that any of these moments would have seemed charged with particular meaning to the casual observer. Revelation refers, not to the quality of an event in and of itself, but rather alludes to an intrapsychic transformation, to a modification in one's deepest understanding, that is associated with that event. It is not simply that the event is revelatory; it is that some individual or group experiences it as such.[15]

The event in itself may be negative, a shattering of meaning. Understandably, that was the initial effect of the death camp for Wiesel, yet this experience served as a major point of reference in the development of his post-Auschwitz sense of purpose. The revelatory event, moreover, does not necessarily contain the whole meaning of one's internal history, for the individual does not always receive full understanding in some blinding flash of insight. One suspects that even the Buddha did not fully appreciate the meaning of his enlightenment during those nights under the bodhi tree.

Revelation alludes to a moment of insight that enables individuals to work out meanings, some of which may be seen, in hindsight, to have been implicit in the event. Revelation seldom gives a complete picture; more often it is the recognition of a clue that helps one in the struggle to build an image. It is an insight that increasingly shapes the story. Gandhi's vivid encounter with his father initially revealed only the depth of parental love, but over time, it emerged in full power to shape the Mahatma's life. That dreadful first night in the death camp forever scarred the life of Elie Wiesel, but as revealed in his later writings, its full meaning took shape as he struggled to see it in a larger context.[16] Tolstoy spent the rest of his life working out the full meaning of that fable.

Moreover, the story that is illuminated is not confined to one's past; revelation becomes a clue for understanding the present and the future. Drawing upon the past, one builds dreams of the future, writing scenarios of that which is yet to be.

One's view of the present is thereby modified.

Religions tell, not only world-defining stories of the past in their creation narratives, but also tales of the future in their eschatological myths, their stories of the end of time. In *The Color Purple*, Celie has that moment of self-discovery when she defies her husband. In response to his taunt that she is nothing, Celie states that she may be a poor Black woman, but that she is nonetheless real.[17] From that moment, she begins a new adventure. Although dependent on Shug at first, she grows in self-confidence until she claims her inheritance, the property left for her and Nettie by her real daddy. She dreams of the day Nettie will come home, bringing Celie's children with her.

Why do we express our faith in stories? Because faith *is* a story. It tells of our discovery of who we are. It tells of our coming to believe in whatever god or gods we worship.

> *The same night he got up and took his two wives, his two maids, and his eleven children, and crossed the ford of the Jab'bok. He took them and sent them across the stream, and likewise everything that he had. Jacob was left alone; and a man wrestled with him until daybreak. When the man saw that he did not prevail against Jacob, he struck him on the hip socket; and Jacob's hip was put out of joint as he wrestled with him. Then he said, "Let me go, for the day is breaking." But Jacob said, "I will not let you go, unless you bless me." So he said to him, "What is your name?" And he said, "Jacob." Then the man said, "You shall no longer be called Jacob, but Israel, for you have striven with God and with humans, and have prevailed." Then Jacob asked him, "Please tell me your name." But he said, "Why is it that you ask my name?" And there he*

blessed him. So Jacob called the place Peniel, saying, "For I have seen God face to face, and yet my life is preserved." The sun rose upon him as he passed Penuel, limping because of his hip. Therefore to this day the Israelites do not eat the thigh muscle that is on the hip socket, because he struck Jacob on the hip socket at the thigh muscle (Gen. 32:22-32, NRSV).

CHAPTER THREE

When Stories Happen to Us

Stories, I remarked earlier, evoke the Child in us. They quicken our sense of wonder, celebration, and playful participation. Being caught up in a good story, being mesmerized by some spinner of tales, has the power to change both us and the way we think, at least while under the spell. Each of these leads on to yet other reasons as to why religious folk tell stories.

Narrative and the Nature of God-Talk: How We Think Religiously

Whether God is called Yahweh, Brahma, Allah, or Gitchi Manitou, these names are believed to point to a special kind of reality. While usually understood as actively involved in everyday life, the divine is also thought of as totally other, lying in the realm of the supernatural, the world of mystery. God is not simply one more thing making up our world; God is an altogether different kind of reality.

For many people today, however, talk of mystery or the supernatural arouses suspicion. Too often, believers seem to others to invoke the mysterious character of their god(s) as a screen to hide confused thinking and uncritical piety. The terms "mysterious" and "supernatural" appear to be used to obscure the fact that god-talk is really meaningless. The word "hocus-pocus," meaning trickery, is symptomatic. It is a corruption of the Latin, *hoc est corpus meum* (this is my body), reflecting a popular feeling in medieval Europe regarding the mass. It was a divine "mystery." Incomprehensible to the faithful, it was simply to be accepted without question on the authority of the Church. To many of our contemporaries, however, to speak of divine mystery in this manner sounds like special pleading. The faithful seem to be claiming a secret source of knowledge. For those outside the faith, all of this lacks the ring of truth.

How then should we understand mystery? Can we give it a significant meaning? Some years ago Gabriel Marcel distinguished between *problems* and *mysteries*.[1] Problems may for a time baffle us; they may be complex and confusing. Ideally, however, they can be solved. That is to say, they can be fully comprehended and explained. Legionnaires' Disease, which caused such concern in Philadelphia in 1976, was eventually understood and the problem solved. Science in general probes matters of this type, though not all, of course, are medical problems. (Nor do all medical problems end in a cure, though they can ideally at least be fully understood.)

While the cause and treatment of various diseases are problems to be tackled by the scientific community, some of the challenges we face are not problems in this sense. For instance, the question as to why we are destined to die despite the best efforts of science does not lend itself to scientific solution. We may, of course, come to a fuller comprehension of the processes of ageing, but that will not "solve" the "problem" of death. A residue will always remain unanswered by such scientific investigations. Were a family member to die in a plane crash, the tragedy (as problem) might be explained in terms of pilot error or equipment failure. Were a healthy young adult to succumb to some strange sickness, a *post mortem* investigation might detect a new virus. In neither instance would that silence the questioning heart. Why did my brother, sister, son, daughter die in this way? What does it mean to live in a world where someday I, and everyone I love, will be dead? What does it mean to live on a planet where the human race may become extinct? Why are we mortal?

Such questions are not subject to scientific answers. They constitute, not problems, but mysteries. We cannot dissolve the disturbing clouds of suffering and death in our experience, leaving behind only an idyllic, clear blue sky of life. Witnessing to the mysterious in the question of evil, there will always be a residue, an undissolved shadow, a dimension to our "Why?" that does not yield a rational explanation.

Let me give a very different example. Most religions tell creation narratives, stories of how the world came to be. Today, such tales are correctly deemed unscientific. Unfortunately, often they are also branded false or foolish. Yet creation narratives were not told to clarify the issues investigated by science, but to explore creation as mystery, rather than as problem.[2]

In his book *The First Three Minutes,*[3] Steven Weinberg assumes a Big Bang origin for the cosmos and speculates on what probably happened during the first moments of its creation. We need not concern ourselves with the details of his account. For our purposes, the important point is that he does not start his account "in the beginning" at time 0 but at time 0.1 seconds. Why? Because such are the limits of science. Drawing upon their knowledge of physics, chemistry, astronomy, scientists try to surmise the processes that brought our present universe into being. They trace the prior history of the universe. Scientific reasoning works within the world order as we know it, and Weinberg's speculations are based on laws of nature operating in the existing universe. Yet the event that started the whole cosmic process stands outside of, because it is prior to, the existing universe and its laws. It is thus beyond the limits of the scientific method. Scientists, as scientists, can say nothing concerning how it all began in an absolute sense. In Marcel's terms, we have entered the realm of mystery, a sphere to which speech can point but words can never capture.

To speak of mystery does not mean, however, being trapped in a realm without light or guidance. Marcel expanded his argument in a simple but helpful way. He drew a distinction between mysteries of light and mysteries of darkness. For some, the honest encounter with suffering and death yields no meaning, but only deeper bewilderment, frustration, and despair. All attempts to understand, all sacrifices made in the fight with evil, seem only to make the cloud darker, the opaqueness more impenetrable. This is to experience suffering and death as a mystery of darkness. None of the world's major religions offers such a bleak picture, though one does find it, for example, in the stark cynicism of a story-teller such as Kafka. Others, by struggling with the problem of suffering, as in the Job and Buddha stories, achieve a deeper comprehension. This allows them to live creatively in the face of that which remains beyond full intellectual mastery or effective control. Such are mysteries of light. While the answer never becomes clear, it becomes less opaque to the human heart.

Whether mysteries of darkness or light, our orientation is not one of detached observation leading to intellectual mastery and control. Rather, we struggle with reality; we enter into its depths; we participate in the pain of suffering and the awesome threat of death. We seek to comprehend by contemplation rather than investigation, by "standing under" rather than by understanding.

Insofar as stories invite participation rather than mastery, they reflect a kinship with the orientation of mystery. They suggest—to a degree—what it means for the faithful person to "know" the sacred. In using stories, the believer is saying, "I cannot capture what I am talking about; I cannot control or master it with my concepts and categories. But I have experienced something of its reality. I have encountered God." Telling the story may serve as a reminder to oneself and as an invitation to others to know the experience behind the tale. In that sense, W. C. Smith can endorse the saying: "Religion is poetry plus, not science minus."[4]

Summarily, to speak of "God" is to speak of a mystery that carries both thought and language beyond themselves. A number of thinkers have pressed this point. When Paul Tillich argued that God does not *exist*, he meant that God is always the "God beyond God," beyond all our language about God, indeed, a reality beyond our power to conceive. Speaking from a specifically Christian context, Urban T. Holmes quotes the words of the Indian shaman who was Castaneda's teacher: "It is only when one claims to understand, that he is really 'in a mess.'"[5] Rubem Alves makes a similar observation in a deliberately provocative way: "The theologian does not have permission to speak the truth," and "that which they produce with their thoughts and words is always less than [truth], [it is] the contemplation of the horizons of eternity."[6]

The philosopher Wittgenstein believed that we must be silent about all that genuinely matters, because we cannot really speak of it. However, religious men and women have not found silence an adequate response, even though they have made room for it in their mystical traditions. I suggest that they have found a way past silence through story. Narrative, I believe, is a form of thinking and speaking especially suited to realities that we cannot control conceptually, that we cannot capture with our words and images. Let me suggest why this is so.

Important insights concerning stories have emerged in the current debates regarding the parables of Jesus. Traditionally, the Good Samaritan has been interpreted as an example-story. The tale offers a picture of goodness, with its purpose reflected in the words, "Go and do likewise." According to John Dominic Crossan, however, the parable was told actually to startle the listener. Christ was questioning the first-century, Jewish assumptions concerning who was good and who was bad. It was told, not to offer a picture of virtue, but to challenge the accepted version. "If the story really intended to encourage help to one's neighbor in distress or even to one's enemy in need, would it not have been much better *to have a wounded Samaritan in that ditch and a Jew stop to aid him?*"[7] We need not delve further into these New Testament debates, but I wish to point out that here one story is seen to have two quite opposite effects: *affirmation,* which offers a picture of reality (in this case a model of goodness), and *disruption,* which challenges that picture. All stories, I suggest, have these attributes.

Narratives offer us (directly or by implication) a way to think about the world. Whatever the intention of the story-teller, their tales invite us to experience things from a particular perspective, to worship certain gods, to adopt certain heroes, to accept certain values. The parable of the Good Samaritan may have been told to shake people up, as Crossan implies, but inevitably it offers an image of goodness. It presents an affirmative, not merely a disruptive, thought.

Some stories are told primarily with a disruptive intent. However, given the powers we have already recognized in narrative experience, I would claim that all stories are potentially disruptive. Elsewhere I have written that stories

> *encourage us to enter their world.... We are lifted out of ourselves and our setting. For the moment we experience another perspective, another possibility which in itself reminds us that ours is not the only one.... Narrative can ignite the imagination.... We are enabled to dream dreams, imagine new possibilities, try new roles, dare to be different. Best of all, stories awaken the child in us; they awaken wonder, fantasy and play. They free us to "sit loose" to the whole thing, to restore the world [as a form of play].[8]*

In short, stories give us an interpretation of reality, a world to live in, but they also invite us to play with that reality. We are encouraged to enter into that world, and, if it seems wise, to alter our understanding of the story and thereby of reality. Narrative experience, the telling and hearing of stories, is at one and the same time affirmative *and* disruptive.

We have now come full circle in our discussion of story and the mysterious nature of religious language. We cited Castaneda's shaman teacher who stated that we really get into trouble when we claim to understand. We noted Wittgenstein's assertion that we must be silent about things that really matter. To this we say, story is the religious way beyond silence. The affirmative and disruptive character of narrative suggests why this is so. By speaking of the sacred in stories, religious persons confess their faith. Yet they do so in a manner that declares that one must go beyond the spoken word to a deeper meaning, one which will always escape our ability to express it.

As Crossan suggests, only when stories carry us beyond the order and meaning we presume to have mastered are we open to encounter and know, to a degree, that which is truly transcendent. Parables "give God room." Stories "shatter the deep structure of our accepted world and thereby render clear and evident to us the relativity of story itself. They remove our defenses and make us vulnerable to God."[9] Story is but a vehicle leading towards truth; it is not that truth. Here the medium cries out that it is *not* the message. If correct, this has profound implications for theology, for our God-talk.

Story-telling, Transformation, and Healing: How We Are Changed

Religions are much more than intellectual systems providing insights into the divine. They claim to offer ultimate fulfilment (heaven, nirvana, the Kingdom of God). To the faithful, the formative and transformative impact of faith is primary. They are not concerned about conceptual systems. Indeed, a religion can exercise such power even though full comprehension of the tradition is beyond one's capabilities. Speaking in the context of the Sufi tradition, Idries Shah writes:

> *The way in which the Master teaches is often incomprehensible to the students. This is generally because they are trying to understand the workings of something when in reality they are in urgent need of*

*its benefits. Without its benefits they will never be able
to understand its workings.*[10]

In a similar vein, Luther's disciple Melanchthon declares that to know Christ is to know his saving benefits. It follows that if story is crucial in the transmission of faith, then story-telling must have some tie to this transformative impact. Let me explore three aspects of that relationship. The first expands on what we saw in the previous chapter concerning our sense of identity. The second gives examples of the therapeutic power of stories. The third offers some insight into why this happens.

Narrative Identity and Therapy. Individuals and groups understand themselves in terms of a personal history, usually enriched by a variety of narratives. Freud thought primarily in terms of memories and fantasies from early childhood that continued to exert influence from the unconscious. He saw the task of therapy as assisting patients to bring such material to consciousness, thus enabling them to deal more adequately with their continuing disruptive effects. To over-simplify, patients must learn to tell themselves different stories.

Eric Berne drew popular attention when he spoke of individuals following "scripts." According to Berne, children make decisions about themselves, their heroes, and the world, and these set the pattern for their later lives. The scripts become self-fulfilling prophecies. The task of therapy is to re-write them. In Berne's picturesque words, the challenge is "to close the show and put a better one on the road."[11]

In keeping with this understanding of the formative role of narrative, pathology (from a psychotherapeutic perspective) may be said to lie in a false or inadequate and repetitive story that distorts a person's perception. The problem is in the "representation of the world and not in the world itself."[12] Thus psychotherapeutic experience teaches that healing requires a new interpretation of reality, a deep exploration leading to a re-writing of the story concerning the self and the world. An inadequate story can be crippling. Narrative has the ability to order life creatively and to heal, but an equal capacity to order life destructively and thus to wound, even to kill.

Obviously, from a social or ethical perspective, such a view must be qualified. We must not be simplistic. If the problem is said to lie primarily in the interpretation of reality, then the appropriate response would be adjustment, not rebellion, and we can understand why therapy has mistakenly been seen as an instrument of the status quo, encouraging adaptation and con-formity. But were we really to tell the black majority of South Africa that they must learn to adjust to apartheid? Was the problem the failure of European Jews to adapt to the racial dream of Nazism? Were our argument to lead to such conclu-sions, the position would be morally repugnant and counter to the ethical imperatives found in most religious traditions. A closer examination of the relationship of identity to therapy, however, leads to a more creative interpretation.

Societies and nations also live in stories, and a word must be said about this. They too understand themselves and their world in terms of a selective past and shared heroes. Psycho-therapists, of course, work with individuals (or small groups) and conceptualize mainly in terms of personal problems. The structure of psychotherapeutic experience and its relation to identity, however, allow us to recognize that a problem may lie not in the individual but in the communal perception of reality. The problem of South African apartheid lay in its representation of reality. That faulty representation, however, was not in the inability of Blacks to come to terms with the dominant political reality, but in the persistent, distorted worldview of the

Afrkaaners' shared identity. The difficulty arose from misdirection, created through their self-image of a people struggling to preserve Christian civilization while surrounded by savage masses. Acknowledging that nations and cultures, as well as individuals, live in their stories allows us to apply therapeutic insights without adopting a socially and ethically irresponsible posture.

To complete this section on the relationship of stories and therapy: when using narratives, therapists have tended to focus upon the ability of story to convey crucial insights. Therapist Joanne Bernstein, for instance, uses stories as a form of vicarious experience to help children cope with death.[13] Their healing potential depends on their dramatic ability to capture fundamental clues concerning the human situation. Indeed, the great figures of literature, Shakespeare, Dostoevsky, Goethe, provide us with more than entertainment; they expand our understanding of ourselves and our world.

Stories have a unique quality that enhances their power to convey such insights. While Freud saw a portrayal of basic familial conflicts operating deep in the human psyche in the saga of *Oedipus Rex*, later theorists, drawing upon the same classic, have discerned very different messages concerning the human dilemma. This diversity points to yet another source of narrative's Therapeutic potential. A single tale can convey many different meanings, a capacity derived from our freedom to play with it. Dylan Thomas saw this openness to new meanings as an important part of the writer's art. "The best craftsmanship," he wrote, "always leaves holes and gaps in the works of the poem so that something that is *not* in the poem can creep, crawl, flash or thunder in."[14] Therapists, in fact, often deliberately construct their tales to leave such gaps.

Narrative then is a powerful means of transformation, for

weal or woe; through it people understand and *mis*understand themselves and reality. Religion uses stories to address the point at which the misunderstanding occurs: the dreams, the heroes, the fears and images that guide the way men and women live and die. Story offers the possibility of healing through its power to suggest new, more humane and creative ways to perceive ourselves, our people, and the shared world.[15]

Fantasy as Therapeutic. Freud, the founder of the modern psychotherapeutic movement, was a champion of rational thinking. He dismissed fantasy as a juvenile vestige to be eradicated, arguing that one must replace the non-rational and wish-dominated thought characterizing childhood, neurosis, and the unconscious. Recently, however, therapists have shown an increased interest in the power and appropriate place of fantasy in adult life. Celia Coates speaks of this as the "re-enchantment of psychotherapy."[16]

Therapists employ fantasy in both a passive and active manner. Ira Progoff, for instance, calls upon his patients to observe passively the images that spontaneously form before their mind's eye. He refers to this as "twilight imagery."[17] Conversely, Frederick Perls, a once-popular Gestalt psychologist, invited people to play roles taken from their dreams. A woman, for example, describes a lake slowly drying up, with creatures stumbling about waiting to die and, finally, an old license plate at the bottom of the lake. Perls asked her to visualize herself as that license plate and tell her story, to expand on this part of her dream.

Let me emphasize that I am speaking of fantasy in its most unrestrained sense. Patients could be asked to imagine themselves paddling a canoe through their own veins and arteries until they come to the source of pain that is then visualized as diminishing. They may even engage in a "conversation" with a failing heart or kidney. Such non-rational methodologies can be highly effective. Augusta Jellinek reports treating a twenty-four-year-old doctoral student in atomic physics who was afflicted with stuttering. The patient was unable to slow down his rate of speech for fear that "it would catch me." He was told to visualize "it" and finally saw a dwarf sitting on his shoulder. Jellinek told him that if he would slow down, the dwarf would starve to death, and he would be free of his stutter. "This extremely intelligent boy understood very well that here he did not deal with rational processes, but with another psychic category."[18] Nevertheless, he was cured of his stuttering. Carl and Stephanie Simonton report similar results using fantasy and imaging when working with cancer patients.[19]

What does one make of this process? As a potent means of direction, it allows us to circumvent the mind's critical functions. Nonetheless, to restrict the power of fantasy to conveying information is to miss an important dimension. Imagination permits us to envision the radically new. Fantasy frees us from the rigid structures of the given and the possible to dream the seemingly impossible.

We have already asserted that in simultaneously affirming and disrupting, narrative carries us beyond silence when confronted by the mystery of things that really matter. We discover a mode of speech that transcends the very words through which it is delivered. Yet imaginative freedom in narrative experience has implications for far more than the way we express ideas. It is also suggestive concerning the therapeutic power of stories. The Child within may need to lead, not only in terms of understanding, but also in relation to healing. Story may be religious and healing because, as fantasy, it is the mind at play.

Story and Therapeutic Freedom. Our reflections upon fantasy suggest that an experience of freedom is essential for the transformation achieved in psychotherapy. That conclusion is, in fact, supported by a variety of practitioners. D. W. Winnicott, for instance, associates psychological healing with the creativity of play.

> *The general principle seems to me to be valid that* psychotherapy is done in the overlap of two play areas, that of the patient and that of the therapist.... *The reason why playing is essential is that it is in playing that the patient is being creative.*[20]

Similarly, Ira Progoff notes that when patients become self-conscious and analytical about their fantasies, the latter lose their power. Thus he calls for psyche-evoking fantasy, replacing rational criticism with the unrestricted play of imagination and opening yet further depths of the mind.[21] Creative power comes with freedom from the limitations of what is taken as reality.

The creative power found in therapeutic fantasy finds a parallel creativity at the communal level. All societies develop structures and conventions to help organize the human world. To be without order is to experience chaos and profound anxiety.[22] Victor Turner, however, posits an intermediate possibility he terms *communitas*, meaning a reality beyond the defined limits of a social order that restricts us to particular roles and status. Yet communitas is not chaotic. Rather, it represents a dynamic flow of human relationships. As Turner sees it, it offers us a richer form of communal existence, a more humane society, even if only for that passing instant of freedom. In that moment, rather than totally rejecting accepted social definitions, we transcend them to experience a new form of community. We are thereby liberated to envisage a new social order. We experience a sociality beyond society, a community that is also communion.[23]

If Turner is correct, social experience, as well as therapy, clearly proclaims a liberating, healing power in the freedom to play, to sit loose to the order and structures of reality. To dream is not to be idle. To engage in fantasy is not to deny harsh reality. To experience again a child-like freedom may carry the seeds of healing (even physical healing) as well as truth.

That moment of playful liberty, however, must stand in relation to some order. From the therapeutic perspective, Winnicott has written, "If the patient cannot play, then something needs to be done to enable the patient to become able to play, after which psychotherapy may begin."[24] It may be necessary to assist individuals to develop a clearer sense of identity, a defining structure, before they feel secure enough to risk playing. At the societal level, the creative moment of communitas described by Turner must stand in relation to some cultural order without which group life would be chaotic. It would seem we need to have structures for transformation as well as for understanding: yet we must be free to move beyond and even to risk their disruption. We need to break out of limiting (though comfortable) understandings and life-styles if we are to be truly creative and alive, if we are to be made whole. We must live by the spirit, not by the letter. This spirit is expressed in these two lines of poetry:

> *Ruffle the perfect manners of the frozen heart,*
> *And compel it once again to be awkward and alive.*[25]

Believers require a framework to guide them in the journey of faith. Without a vision, there is only confusion. Thus the Buddhist sets out on the Eightfold Path, the Hindu practises the way of Yoga, the Jew seeks guidance in the Torah, the Christian endeavours to imitate Christ. But ultimate transformation requires freedom to transcend these patterns, these religious ways of understanding the meaning of life. Insofar as the presentation of such visions does not invite the faithful to look beyond the words presented, it will fail to bear witness to the truth it would proclaim. Insofar as it tends to absolutize the accepted form and expression, it will not foster the religious transformation it claims to serve. Language can at best point the way. Religious communication, to be truthful and healing, must call the faithful to go beyond its words and images, and for this it turns to stories.

A rabbi whose grandfather had been a disciple of the Baal Shem Tov told this story:

> *One day my grandfather was asked to tell some stories about his master. He recounted how, whenever the Baal Shem Tov prayed, he would be carried away in ecstasy and begin to hop and dance. My grandfather was lame. Yet as he told the story, he stood up and began to hop and dance as had his beloved teacher. From that moment, he was no longer lame. That's the way to tell stories.*

Part Three:
The Stories of Faith

What do I mean by "story"? I use the term broadly. For me, a story is the relating of a sequence of events, real or fictional, in a connected narrative, in an account with a story-line or plot. As such, I include the whole spectrum, from the most fanciful myths to factual history. All are represented among the accounts cherished by women and men of faith. Given this vast range, we must develop a scheme for organizing the material. We need some pegs on which to hang our various narrative hats. That will put us in a position to move from talking about stories to the delight of sharing some, knowing what kind of stories we are hearing. At each peg-point, I shall include an example-story taken from the Christian tradition, as well as one or more from another faith.

Religious tales range from fantastic myths to homey examples from everyday life. Christians will recognize the well-known story of Jesus' miraculous calming of the Sea of Galilee. (Artist's interpretation of a detail from The Stilling of the Tempest *by Monika Lin Ho-Peh.)*

CHAPTER FOUR

What Goes Where?

The briefest survey of religion reveals that the faithful tell many kinds of stories. Indeed we can easily be overwhelmed by their sheer volume and variety. We must be able to distinguish, for instance, between Dickens' *A Christmas Carol* and the various, often fanciful, lives of St. Francis as narrative types. How are they alike? How do they differ? Effective analysis requires a systematic way to compare such obviously diverse stories as the creation narratives in Genesis, the "biography" of David in Kings, the "record" of Holy Week, the story of the Good Samaritan, and the vision offered in The Revelation of John. When we add to this the tales cherished in Hinduism or Islam, to mention only two other faiths, we have indeed a vast array.

I propose to classify faith stories by asking three questions. Taken together, our answers will provide a framework for ordering the world of religious narratives. Obviously the characters and events in Hindu tales differ widely from those recounted in the Bible, and both may seem very unlike the faith stories told in the Iroquois long house tradition. That said, it remains important to detect when such Hindu, Christian, and First Nation accounts are the same type of narrative. One can develop many such schemes. The crucial issue is to ask the right questions, to develop the right categories. The value of any scheme depends upon the usefulness of the insights derived. With this caveat, I offer mine. I have prepared a chart to summarize this chapter. You will find it on page 57.

My first classification relates to the part a given story plays in conveying the community's religious vision: What is its role? The second classification employs a purely literary distinction: What is the setting for the story? The last classification enquires as to its theme: What is the story about? (The latter two will prove important when we address the question of truth.)

What Is the Role of the Story?

I suggest that stories play one of four basic roles: world-defining, world-defending, world-illustrating, and world-disrupting. What is the meaning of "world" in this context? Clearly, I am not saying that the telling of a story literally determines the laws of nature as they exist out there. Nor does it defend the continued existence of such a natural order. Nor is it capable of disrupting such laws. By "world" I mean, not the world in itself, but the human perception of that world, a community's world-taken-for-granted. I have in mind human presuppositions concerning reality. I think of basic convictions about meaning and values that regulate communal life.

World-defining stories, then, are the narrative accounts that set forth this basic and definitive understanding. They give to a

community a sense of reality, a world in which to live. Hugh
Kenner makes the point with poetic force.

> *Whoever can give his people better stories than the
> ones they live in is like the priest in whose hands
> common bread and wine become capable of feeding the
> very soul, and he may think of forging in some
> invisible smithy the uncreated conscience of his race.*[1]

This category of world-defining stories correlates readily
with our insights concerning religion and identity formation.
We understand the world and ourselves in terms of a story. The
Exodus-Sinai narrative is an example of such a story. The
Hebrews believed in an Exodus God and lived in a world where
an Exodus was always possible.

As the name implies, *world-defending stories* are told to
support a community's vision of reality. Tales of heroic figures,
especially those of key players in the world-defining narrative,
frequently fill this role. They "verify" the heroic figure's credentials, underlining his or her claim to be taken seriously. (The
mothers of both Jesus and the Buddha are said to have conceived
miraculously.) Similarly, crucial episodes in the world-defining
story may take on miraculous proportions as in the Red Sea
crossing. Yet the supernatural character of the events recounted
is not the primary message. The tale is meant to substantiate the
defining character of the event and thus a community's world-
taken-for-granted.

World-illustrating stories portray life in that world, either in
its ideal form or as it is usually experienced. Some hero stories
present their champions as ideals for the faithful. They model
the life to which believers are called. (The Hebrew sagas of
Joseph and of David are, in part at least, heroic narratives of this

latter type.) Other world-illustrating stories offer not models of goodness but, rather, images of ordinary men and women, dramatic representations of the essential human situation in its beauty and ugliness, goodness and evil, triumphs and defeats. The classic allegory *Pilgrim's Progress* is an example of such, as are most of Jesus' parables.

Summarily, then, world-defining stories set forth a community's basic vision of reality and include the great religious myths, as well as the definitive memories of the significant moments in a people's history. World-defending stories are tales intended to support the credentials of central figures or to emphasize the importance of moments in the world-defining narrative. World-illustrating stories offer insights into the nature of life and our spiritual pilgrimage, either by presenting heroes to be emulated or by offering scenes from the life of ordinary folk.

Before moving to the fourth category, it will help to note that the latter two categories differ significantly from the first. To reject a world-defining story is to repudiate the faith tradition. This does not mean, of course, that we take all such stories as literally true. Nonetheless, to say that God did not create the heavens and the earth or that God was not in Christ or was not revealed to humanity through Mohammed would be to reject or radically alter Christianity or Islam. On the other hand, one may feel unable to accept particular world-defending or world-illustrating stories and not thereby repudiate the basic tradition. For some, to omit the virgin birth from the Christian story would mean the loss of dramatic support for the divinity of Christ, but it would not mean one must reject that claim. Indeed, two of the Gospels make no reference to the birth of Jesus. In a similar way, the loss of any particular story of a brahmin's many cycles of life would not amount to a denial of the reality of reincarnation.

World-disrupting stories, our final class, are told to challenge or subvert the established worldview. They oppose the faith tradition witnessed to in our first three classes. World-disrupting stories, as used here, denotes narratives that challenge the existing religious vision without presenting an alternative. Witness the saga of Jonah, which questions the Hebrews' basic assumption concerning the meaning of Israel's election. Nineveh was not merely non-Israelite; it stood for the great empires of the East that had so long oppressed the "chosen people." Yet God wished to save Nineveh. A disturbing thought for a chosen people! (Disruption may also come, of course, through an encounter with a competing world-defining story, an increasingly common experience in today's highly pluralistic society.)

What Is the Setting for the Story?

Narrative setting is the distinguishing factor in our second classification. Here we find a spectrum that runs from the fabulous to the ordinary, from the most remote to that which seems entirely continuous with our experience. At the one extreme lies *myth,* a recounting of events outside our space and/or time, outside the world of history. Some tell of events "in the beginning." Some tell of the end of time. Others take place outside our world, in a supernatural realm, though at a time concurrent with our history. One thinks here of the many tales in Greek mythology.[2] At the opposite end of the spectrum, some stories relate actual events as they take place in our world. These I designate as *history-biography.*

One step closer to our world than myth, and one degree less fabulous, are *legends.* These describe events within our space and time that include the appearance of realities coming from beyond it. They tell of supernatural incursions into the natural. Myth may tell of a cosmic battle beyond the stars in which the deity slays the monster of the great deep and builds a world from its body. History speaks of the clash of armies at Waterloo or Gettysburg; it chronicles the struggles between the kings and generals of this world, striving for political and economic advantage. In legend, the battle still takes place in our world but the armies include gods and demons, supernatural realities from beyond our space and/or time. Anything can happen in myth because the structures of our world and the laws of nature do not apply. We may be surprised by events in history, but we nonetheless recognize our world with its laws of nature. This order remains as the basic framework in legend, but for a moment, it may miraculously be set aside. At the bidding of a holy man, an icicle may burn as a candle. As an answer to prayer, the sun may cease to move, providing sufficient daylight for the lost to find their way.

The first step away from our ordinary world, from history, brings us to the general class of *ordinary fiction*. Here imaginary, natural events, moments in our everyday world, are recounted. They differ from history only in the fact that they did not occur.

What Is the Story About?

The literary test governing our third set of categories hardly needs explanation. Stories are grouped in terms of broad, general themes. We find, for instance, creation narratives, dramatic visions of the end of the world, and heroic models of virtuous living.

So much for my scheme. We are now ready to use it to build a framework in which to place a rich variety of tales from numerous faith traditions. It's time for some stories! Initially, I shall use my first and last classifications to form the primary organization. We shall explore the basic themes expressed in our world-defining, world-defending, and world-illustrating stories. World-disrupting stories, as I have said, do not offer an alternative vision; they simply challenge the existing view. Thus, in that case, thematic variations will not play a significant role. All four functional types, however, employ narratives in a variety of settings. World-defining tales of healing, for example, can be further divided into mythical, legendary, fictional, and historical accounts.

The next chapter will focus upon world-defining stories. These form the heart of any tradition; they constitute the Great Story of the faith, that which sets forth a people's fundamental religious vision. Here one explores life at its deepest. What is its meaning? Dare we trust whomever or whatever it was that brought us and our world into being? What is good? For whom or what should one even be willing to die? What is our hope? To reject such a story is to reject or radically alter the faith. We shall explore themes of world-defining stories and their various modes of expression in myth, legend, ordinary fiction, and history-biography.

The following chapter will offer examples of world-defending, world-illustrating, and world-disrupting stories. These nurture the human spirit by supporting, illustrating, and sometimes challenging the vision proclaimed in the Great Story.

Let us be clear as to what we have tried to accomplish here. Classification of stories by role, setting, and theme does not settle the question of truth. Was God in Christ? Was the Qur'an dictated to Mohammed by the archangel Gabriel? Did the Buddha discover the Truth as he sat under that bodhi tree? These are matters for future consideration. At the moment, I am offering a way to organize our religious narratives. The critical question at this point is whether that structure proves useful, whether it throws light upon the vast sea of faith-full stories.

The Sufi tradition of Islam contains many stories about the Mulla Nasrudin, a wise, whimsical fool. Here is one.

> *One day a man discovered Nasrudin on his knees, searching for something on the ground. "What are you missing, Mulla?", he asked. "My key," came the reply. So the other joined him in feeling about for the lost key. After some time of fruitless searching, he inquired, "Where exactly were you when you dropped it?" "In my house," he muttered. "Then why are we looking out here?" "The light is better here," the Mulla replied, as if that were obvious.*

The Story Chart

Role	Theme	SETTING			
		Myth	Legend	Natural Fiction	History-Biography
World-Defining Stories	Creation: How and why there is a world	Genesis 1-2 P'an Ku		Coyote plants seed—food for the human race to come*	
	The Problem: What is wrong and why	Marduk makes humanity mortal and weak		Evil mountain goat mixes white sand with red clay in Coyote's magic bag, which means two races will come, and tension	
	Stories of Transformation: How what is wrong is put right	Christ defeats Satan in cosmic battle Hindu cycle of existence	Easter*	Roar of Awakening	Passion Narrative The Enlightenment of Buddha Easter*

Role	Theme	Myth	Legend	Natural Fiction	History-Biography
World-Defining Stories	Visions of the End	Revelation 14-22	Easter* Coyote and Old Man	Dives and Lazarus Divine Comedy	Easter*
World-Illustrating Stories	The Hero's Credentials	Pre-existence of Christ Jesus before Bethlehem	Miraculous Birth of Jesus, Buddha, Abraham Mohammad's trip to heaven	Krishna charms 1,000 maidens with his dancing	David and Goliath Boy Jesus in the temple
	This event was important/revelatory		Red Sea Miracle		Centurion's confession as Jesus dies: "This man was a son of God"

Role	Theme	Myth	Legend	Natural Fiction	History-Biography
World-Illustrating Stories	Models of Virtue	Prose Introduction to Job	Devils torment St. Francis at prayer	Stag-Buddha offers his life for a pregnant doe* Dicken's Christmas Carol	Biographies: e.g., Schweitzer, Gandhi, Mother Theresa
	The Way Things Are		Hindu King goes directly to paradise because he gave his life to protect a dove	Friar Brian saves a man from the devil Prodigal Son	Buddha sends a grieving mother to find mustard seeds from a house where no one has died
World-Disrupting Stories			Ignorant man could not pronounce the chant properly but could walk on water	Good Samaritan	Story of Ruth*

As you see, some squares in the chart have few if any entries. Creation stories, for example, by their very nature tend to take the form of myths. They describe events before there was a world and thus outside our space and time. Similarly accounts of how and why there is evil or a problem in life are normally myths, since it has usually been assumed that the problem existed from the start. Some accounts of Creation and the "Fall," however, do take the form of legends, fiction, or history. These are told as if occurring very early in the history of the world. I have included some of these.

*The decision on where to place some stories depends upon certain critical judgements. The story of Easter is a complex example. It is in part a redemption story and in part an image of individual hope for life beyond death, a vision of the end. It thus appears under two roles. Depending on whether or not one takes it as history or as a poetic statement of faith, it will fall under legend or biography. The story of the Buddha's earlier life as a stag will probably be read by non-Buddhists as fiction. For a devout Buddhist who accepts the reality of reincarnation, the story may be history. The story of Ruth reads like history. If in fact it is not, then it would join the Good Samaritan as fiction.

CHAPTER FIVE

Our Story, Our World

Most world-defining stories contain four chapters, each presenting a different basic theme. The first chapter offers creation narratives, stories which "explain" how and why our world came to be. The second chapter explores the reason for its blighted nature, for sin, death, ignorance, or whatever is seen to be the darkest element in experience. Stories of salvation, healing, and transformation constitute the third chapter. How are things put right? Finally, as humankind has asked about the beginning, so it asks about the end, developing its visions of fulfilment in a final chapter.

Creation Stories: The Time before Time

Creation stories describe the absolute beginning of all things, how and why our world came to be in the first place. They open at a time before time, recording events prior to our world, perhaps to *any* world. Set outside our space and time, they are myths. (Here we make no judgement as to the truth; we simply acknowledge that they are neither history nor science.)

Clearly, the first two chapters of Genesis are creation stories. To be sure, in each instance the story-teller moves quickly to images from the world we know: light, wind, rain, dust. Genesis 1 begins, "In the beginning when God created the heavens and the earth...." As the story opens, neither the heavens nor the earth exist. Soon our sage speaks of "a mighty wind from God [that] swept over the surface of the waters." Yet this is still not our world for it is one without dry land, without day and night, with neither sun nor stars to brighten the sky. The narrative ends with a summary statement that reveals its character: "Thus the heavens and the earth were finished" (Gen. 1-2, *NRSV*).

In the Genesis accounts, God is the creator of the world. Many creation narratives, however, offer a different picture. The supreme god, the Absolute, or some unknown and undefined power first creates a lesser deity or even a first human who creates heaven and earth. The Chinese tell such a story concerning P'an Ku. (It is interesting to note, by the way, that Chairman Mao alluded to P'an Ku in some of his poetry.)

> *At first there was nothing. Time passed and nothing became something. Time passed again and something split in two: they were male and female. These two produced two more who produced P'an Ku, the first being, the Great Man, the Creator.*

One senses in this strange language the attempt to deal with a mystery. An abundance of stories detail the work of P'an Ku. In some he creates order out of primal chaos; in others, he dies that his body may be transformed into the world. (The idea that sacrifice is a necessary part of the creative process is found in many religious traditions.) Here is an example of the latter.

> *The world was only finished when P'an Ku died. Only his death could perfect the universe: from his skull came the dome of the sky, and the soil of the fields was formed from his flesh; his bones became the rocks, his blood the rivers and seas, his hair all vegetation. His breath was the wind; his voice made thunder; his right eye became the moon, and his left, the sun. From his sweat came the rain. And the vermin which covered his body yielded mankind.*

Hinduism offers a variety of creation stories, each describing a two-step process. One account portrays a cyclical creation in which one universe follows another after an interval of rest. The story tells of Brahma, the creator, who owes his existence to the prior action of the supreme deity, Vishnu. In this version, Brahma appears seated on a lotus blossom that arises from Vishnu's navel.

> *Creation came to pass in this way:*
> *Vishnu was brooding on Naga, king of the serpents, as Naga floated upon the waters. The world was still submerged beneath the ocean.*
> *As the time of creation drew nigh, God felt a stirring and a full-blown Lotus issued forth from the centre of his being.*
> *Immediately Brahma came forth from the Lotus, and, seating himself upon it, turned his head in all directions to see whether any other beings were present.*

So he is called the four-faced Brahma.

Looking about him and seeing in the external world no hope to fulfil his desires, he sought in meditation the knowledge which he realized must be within himself, and at last he found the Truth, and God himself, within his own heart.

Then God said: "O Brahma, I command thee: again create the world, as thou hast often done in times past. To create is not new to thee. Whatever is to be created is already within me. This thou knowest well."

Stories of Pain and Evil

Humankind seems never to have found the world entirely to its liking. While some dream of an idyllic past or future, few if any think of themselves as living in a perfect world. And so we find stories exploring what is wrong with the world and who is to blame. These accounts are normally myths. What they describe usually takes place before the world has come to be, or at the dawn of creation, before history has really begun. The negative, it is most often assumed, has always been there.

A comparative reading of these stories reveals important differences between various faiths. In doing so, however, we must strive to hear these stories within their own context and not impose our own; otherwise, we shall not really hear them.

Let us begin in familiar territory with Genesis 3, the biblical myth of the fall. Some Christians have interpreted this as history, recalling the original sin of our "first parents." The difficulties raised by such an interpretation have caused most biblical scholars to regard the passage as myth. But, again, let us remember that the choice between history and myth is not that between truth versus falsehood.

Now the serpent was more crafty than any other wild animal that the Lord God had made. He said to the woman, "Did God say, 'You shall not eat from any tree in the garden'?" The woman said to the serpent, "We may eat of the fruit of the trees in the garden; but God said, 'You shall not eat of the fruit of the tree that is in the middle of the garden, nor shall you touch it, or you shall die.'" But the serpent said to the woman, "You will not die; for God knows that when you eat of it your eyes will be opened, and you will be like God, knowing good and evil." So when the woman saw that the tree was good for food, and that it was a delight to the eyes, and that the tree was to be desired to make one wise, she took of its fruit and ate; and she also gave some to her husband, who was with her, and he ate. Then the eyes of both were opened, and they knew that they were naked; and they sewed fig leaves together and made loincloths for themselves (Gen. 3:1-7, NRSV).

God punishes the serpent, the woman, and the man for this transgression. Clearly, this is the story of a fall; a good creation has been degraded. Humankind has fallen into sin. Yet the figure of the serpent suggests a mysterious depth to sin and implies more than a simple free choice by Adam and Eve. Moreover, the tale also clearly implies that the negative dimensions of life were not inevitable; the world could have remained unspoiled.

In Hinduism, we have a falling away but one which is inevitable. The first chapter, we saw, describes a series of creations. Each universe evolves out of and later is absorbed back into the deity, thereby ending a particular world and era. Initially creation is good and beautiful. Each world begins with a time of happiness, harmony, and all virtues. The great Hindu epic *Mahabharata* describes it thus:

> *No efforts were made by men; the fruit [of the earth] was obtained by their mere wishes. No disease or decline of organs of sense arose through the influence of age; there was no malice, weeping, pride or deceit, no contention, no hatred, cruelty, fear, affliction, jealousy or envy.*

This good creation, however, gradually and inevitably decays. The story then records a progressive deterioration to a final degenerate phase, which is our present age.

> *Men are led by their wives, women become shameless, overbold and lascivious ... kings become oppressive ... householders neglect their duties.... In short, the condition of the world becomes so bad, wise men pray for the arrival of Kalki, the destroyer.*

All of recorded history is seen as part of the final age. The account of the earlier phases becomes a myth that "highlights" our present distress. Creation comes to an end by dissolving into an undifferentiated state, represented by the sea upon which Vishnu and the serpent rest. Decline is thus a part of the very structure of reality. It is a fall, but one bound to happen because of the character of the universe. No blame is assigned.

In Babylonian and Sumerian traditions, the problem is mortality, physical decay, not moral decline. One tale asserts that the curse of mortality is intrinsic to human nature. In this version, the god Marduk slays the sea monster Tiamat, creating the earth and the sky from her body. As a result, he becomes king of the gods, assigning to each a realm in heaven or on earth. While the gods rejoice at Marduk's victory, they also worry lest they be required to work at looking after this new creation. Marduk allays their fear by creating a human race to perform these menial tasks. Moreover, he assures them that these creatures shall remain subservient. The story continues:

> *"They will be weak, no threat to us gods. To prevent them learning our skills in time, or growing strong enough to challenge us, they shall be mortal: after some time, they will die."*
>
> *To create our race, Marduk used the body of a defeated god. After He had cut off the immortal head he fashioned a misshapen, ridiculous copy of the immortal gods. Stumbling and shuffling, the new creature crept off to begin his lowly life. Man was born.*

Not all stories associate the evil dimensions of reality so closely with humanity. The Zoroastrian tradition offers a very different account. The evil at the heart of creation flows from the fact that our world is not the handiwork of a single benevolent god. Instead we find a god of light and goodness, Ahura Mazda, and a god of darkness and evil, Ahriman. For a long time there was no conflict between them, as the two existed separately. Ahriman, in the darkness of ignorance, did not even know of Ahura Mazda. When Ahriman first saw Ahura Mazda surrounded by dazzling brightness, his evil nature compelled him to attack. He forced Ahura Mazda to battle constantly with his destructive powers. Ahura Mazda then proceeded to make the world. That creative effort ends with the appearance of the human race, called to join him in the struggle.

> *Ahura Mazda intended that the descendants of Mashya and Mashyoi [the human race] should live in his kingdom and join him in the long struggle between goodness and evil. In time, however, many joined Ahriman instead and became evil. But the battle will end; a saviour, Soshyant, will be born, and good will finally triumph over evil.*

The closing words of this story point towards yet other stories. These are narratives with a different thematic focus, tales of salvation, how the wrong is rectified, and of the end, our ultimate hope.

Stories of Transformation: How What Is Wrong Is Put Right

We come now to what is arguably the heart of faith's story. Men and women have never been content merely to acknowledge the pain, frustration, and defeats of life. Central to the overall world-defining stories of faith, and of supreme importance, then, is a "drama of redemption," a tale of putting things right.

The Exodus (or, better, the Exodus-Sinai account) is the primary moment in the Hebrew story. The complete narrative as it came to be told very early in Israelite history opens with a creation myth and moves on to recount God's dealings with the Patriarchs. Nevertheless, the escape from Egypt remains the crucial event. The Great Story tells us that, in the midst of history, God acted to save his people. Such is the foundation of Israel's hope. The climax comes, of course, at the Red Sea.

Israelite history chronicles repeated faithlessness to Yahweh and the Covenant, which evoked divine punishment at the hands of other nations. Yet the note of hope remains. An Exodus God means that redemption is always possible. Indeed, in that light, the unknown prophet of the Exile hopes for a return from Babylon. He links the mighty action of God in creation (the reference here to Rahab echoes a Babylonian myth) and the dividing of the waters in the Exodus with hope for a New Exodus, a new saving act. Events and characters from the Great Story appear as images in later forms of that tale.

> *Awake, awake, put on your strength, O arm of the Lord!*
>
> *Awake as in days of old, the generations of long ago.*
>
> *Was it not you who cut Rahab in pieces, who pierced the dragon?*
>
> *Was it not you who dried up the sea, the waters of the great deep, who made the depths of the sea a way for the redeemed to cross over?*
>
> *So the ransomed of the Lord shall return, and come to Zion with singing,*
>
> *everlasting joy shall be upon their heads;*
> *they shall obtain joy and gladness,*
> *and sorrow and sighing shall flee away.*
>
> *(Isa. 51:9-11, NRSV)*

The heart of the Christian narrative (as found in the Gospels and Acts) is likewise a story of redemption. We read of God entering history in the life of Jesus of Nazareth to defeat the enslaving power of sin. In many ways, Christian theology is a continuous attempt to understand the story of that life, especially its final week, which culminates in the crucifixion/resurrection narrative. The interpretations given and the implications derived through the centuries have undergone significant shifts. Nevertheless, the Jesus story is always central and its meaning is salvation. The full world-defining story for Christians, to be sure, draws upon the traditions of Israel. They share with Jews the assumptions of God as creator, the human predicament as basically a moral failure, and the hope that God will act again to redeem his people. However, the story of ultimate transformation remains focused upon Good Friday and Easter.

Unlike Judaism and Christianity, Hinduism contains no incident comparable to the Exodus, nor an individual akin to Jesus. For Hindus, the way to salvation is through enlightenment. The ignorance that holds humanity in bondage is shattered with awareness of one's true divine nature. A popular Hindu fable, "The Roar of Awakening," dramatizes this blindness and the startling moment of self-discovery. A tiger cub, raised by sheep, develops the ways of his foster family. He lives on grass, bleats like a lamb, and is gentle of spirit. One day an old tiger attacks and scatters the flock. The cub is confronted by the intruder, who demands to know why he is living with the sheep. The cub only bleats. Angered, the old tiger drags him to a pond to see them both reflected in the water. Then, taking him to his den, he forces the cub to eat raw meat.

> *The cub began to feel an unfamiliar gratification as the new meal went down his throat, and the meat entered his stomach. A strange, new strength went out through his whole body and he became elated, intoxicated. His lips smacked; he licked his jowls. He arose and yawned mightily, as if he were waking from a deep sleep. Stretching, he arched his back and spread his paws. His*

tail lashed the ground, and suddenly from his throat came the terrifying, triumphant roar of a tiger. Then the old tiger demanded gruffly: "Now do you know who you really are?"

A second facet of the Hindu story is the assertion that religious fulfilment and personal transformation are always possible. The story of cyclical creation, with its assumption of inevitable moral decline, is also a story of hope. The destruction of one age always leads to another. This understanding and hope applies to individual men and women, as well as to the world. *Samsara*, or reincarnation, promises another chance. Various Hindu world-illustrating stories offered in the next chapter enlarge upon this understanding. Indeed, it is by hearing these that the Hindu tale of redemption will really take shape for us.

In the End: Stories of the Last Things

The final chapter in our world-defining stories develops two related themes. One deals with personal destiny, with the aftermath of individual lives, and the other, with the end of the world. In biblical terms, the first theme offers stories of heaven and hell. The second theme describes a new heaven and a new earth that mark the end of the present cosmos and its history.

Virtually all traditions offer some image of the ultimate consequence of how one lives in this world. Almost without exception, one encounters images of reward and punishment, paradise and misery. This world may or may not end, but clearly individual lives do, and the significance of that fact is graphically portrayed. In most traditions, however, the world-defining story of personal destiny tends to be assumed rather than explicitly narrated.

Admittedly, the story of Christ's resurrection and ascension *is* world-defining for Christians, and proclaims the basis for individual hope. Still, in Christianity, as in most traditions, this facet of the Great Story is normally reflected in the presuppositions underlying world-illustrating stories that portray the final destiny of particular men and women. These are world-illustrating rather than world-defining. While they describe reality as pictured by Christians, such stories can be rejected without radically altering the faith. Jesus' parable of the rich man who left poor Lazarus lying at his gate accepts the Christian view of human destiny, but that story could be rejected without changing the essence of faith. In short, the faithful tend to assume, rather than tell, the last chapter of the Great Story as it relates to individuals.

This lesser attention to matters of personal destiny may reflect the fact that religion's primary focus is upon ways of transformation. The concern is not so much with a future heaven or hell as it is with the struggle against sin or illusion here and now. Yet these implicit world-defining stories of personal destiny remain important. To deny the ultimate hope for the individual as proclaimed in any religious tradition would be to change it fundamentally. To assert that death can separate us from the love of God in Christ Jesus or that the hope of nirvana is itself an illusion, would be to alter Christianity or Buddhism significantly.

I need not recount the Christian image of individual destiny. Dante's *Divine Comedy* is a classic example of the tradition. This fourteenth-century work, a visionary journey through Paradise, Purgatory, and Hell, provides graphic images of the joy and blessedness of the redeemed and the terror and suffering of the damned. Hinduism and Buddhism have a similar story, one told against the background of a cyclical creation. According to these traditions, women and men have a series of lives on earth. Between each life, the individual dwells in paradise or hell, depending upon his or her previous incarnation. Beyond this phase lies an ultimate hope, escape from the cycle of rebirth. Hindus called this *moksa* (release); Buddhists, *nirvana*. The Hindu story of King Puramjana illustrates this.

> *The king left his beautiful wife in order to devote himself to unrestrained hunting. Mercilessly he slaughtered deer, boar, and any other beast crossing his path, always deaf to their pitiful cries. Later, tiring of the hunt, he returned to the pleasures of marital bliss.*
>
> *At the moment of his death his thoughts were of his wife and the pain his death would cause her. As a result, Puramjana was reborn a woman—after one hundred years in hell, where he was tormented by the beasts he had abused in his orgy of hunting.*
>
> *In his new life, Puramjana was a devoted wife called Vaidarbhi. Upon the death of her husband, she prepared his funeral pyre and was ready to throw herself upon it when she was stopped by a Brahmin. He reminded her that in a former life, she was Puramjana, the king, and before that a beautiful swan who lived for one thousand years near the city where Puramjana ruled. At once the former swan-Puramjana-Vaidarbhi realized his true nature and was released from the cycle of rebirth.*

And what of the ultimate fate of humankind, the end of history, the destiny of the universe? In the Christian tradition, The Revelation of John tells of a temporary fulfilment within history, which takes the form of the thousand-year reign of the Messiah. Following this, Satan again vents his rage upon humanity. The ultimate comes only with a new creation, purged of sin and graced by the presence of God.

> *When the thousand years are ended, Satan will be released from his prison and will come out to deceive the nations at the four corners of the earth.... And fire came down [on the satanic forces] from heaven and consumed them (Rev. 20:7-9b, NRSV).*

> *Then I saw a new heaven and a new earth; for the first heaven and the first earth had passed away.... And I heard a loud voice from the throne saying, "See, the home of God is among mortals. He will dwell with them as their God; they will be his peoples, and God himself will be with them; he will wipe every tear from their eyes. Death will be no more; mourning and crying and pain will be no more, for the first things have passed away" (Rev. 21:1-4, NRSV).*

Finally, consider this story of the end of time from the traditions of North America's First Nations. It has some similarities to the Christian story of the Second Coming. Coyote, a kind of supernatural Being, was instrumental in creating and in saving the human race. I shall tell the story at some length for it has great charm.

> *Coyote had finished his work. He had conquered Ice and Blizzard. He had destroyed the monsters, killing*

*some and turning others into the harmless creatures
we know, such as marmots and mosquitoes. By putting
salmon in the rivers, he had given food for his people.
He had shown the arts of civilization to make their
lives easier and happier. Now it was time to meet Old
Man.*

*"You must be the Great Chief, Old Man," Coyote
said. "I was looking for you." "I am," he replied. "You
have been here a long time. You have finished your
work. Nothing more must be done. Soon we shall both
leave the earth. But one day you will come again with
me. Again we will change the world and bring the
dead back to the land of the living."*

*Far away, Old Man made a great ice house for
Coyote. Inside was a large log, which would burn
forever and forever, and be warmth for Coyote.*

*One day Coyote and Old Man will return to work
wonders on the earth. At the right time, they will
bring the dead from the Land of Shades. With a loud
beating of drums, the dead will appear, carried on red
clouds, the northern lights, and tobacco smoke.*

Let us reflect for a moment on these world-defining stories.
Although our first reaction may be amusement or scepticism,
these stories are neither false histories nor bad science. They
speak of mysteries, of wonder, of those things that inevitably
carry language beyond its normal use. To grasp their meaning,
we must let them be *story* with all that that entails. We must try
to sense what it would be like if their images had shaped our
deepest understandings. Only then shall we understand the
place of world-defending and world-illustrating stories in supporting and "fleshing out" such visions. Only then shall we
fathom the need for world-disrupting stories.

Chapter Six

Stories about Our Story

In the narrative framework developed in chapter 4, I proposed three other roles for stories. Each of these is in service to the Great Story, the world-defining narrative. Some are recounted to defend its claims; some to illustrate life in such a world; still others to serve by challenging that vision. Let me make this abstract scheme clearer with some concrete examples.

World-Defending Stories

The first line of defence for the shared assumptions of any society is, of course, the very taken-for-granted character of its Great Story. If virtually everyone shares that understanding, it will obviously seem to be true. In practice, however, the community's guiding vision is never taken for granted by everyone. On the fringes of every society are people who do not share its values and assumptions, who live in a different story. (The threat this poses to the dominant community appears throughout history in the form of racial and religious prejudice.)

The claims of the traditional world are not always self-evident to a society's youth, for example. I recall the horror on the face of a father when his daughter angrily challenged him, "Don't tell me not to have sex 'for Jesus' sake.' Give me a good reason." In our terms, she meant that if you already accept the Christian story, if you live with its values and assumptions, then "for Jesus' sake" is enough. But if that story has yet to come alive for you, then you will want reasons to believe, you will need convincing. World-defending stories are told to bolster the claims of a faith tradition's vision. We tell them to win over the outsider and our children, as well as to strengthen our own commitment against the assault of other stories. We can distinguish two types. Some are intended to substantiate the hero's special status. Others are told to show the revelatory character of the world-defining event(s).

Not surprisingly, such tales often seek emphasis by dramatically incorporating supernatural dimensions to stress their point. Thus, they are often legends or at least have legendary characteristics. The hero's birth, for example, may be attributed to supernatural intervention, as in the Christian accounts of Jesus' virgin birth, which was accompanied by an angelic chorus and celestial splendour. The birth of Prince Siddhartha Gautama, who was to become the Buddha, is similarly described.

> *In a dream the four guardian angels carried the Queen, his mother, upon her couch to the Himalayan Mountains. Now the future Buddha had become a magnificent white elephant and was wandering near the Golden Mansion where she lay. Approaching*

from the north and holding a white lotus with his silvery trunk, he trumpeted loudly. Three times he circled, brushing her right side. And so he entered her womb. Thus was the Buddha conceived during the midsummer festival.

Immediately all the ten thousand worlds quivered and shook and a great light spread throughout their vast domain; the blind gained their sight, as if to see his glory; the deaf could hear; the dumb recovered speech; the hunchback became straight; the lame could walk; all the fires of hell were extinguished; wild animals lost their timidity; every musical instrument gave forth its sound though no one played upon it.

Though Abraham was not supernaturally conceived, in Jewish tradition his birth includes divine intervention.

Reading of Abraham's birth in the stars, the evil king orders all male infants slain. As her time drew near, his mother fled to a cave in the desert. There she was seized with pains of childbirth and brought forth a son. The light of the child's countenance filled the cave like the splendour of the sun, and she rejoiced greatly. The child was our father Abraham. Wrapping the babe in her own garment, she prayed, "May the Lord be with thee, may He not fail thee nor forsake thee." So the babe was abandoned.

Being without a nurse, Abraham began to cry. So God sent Gabriel to give him milk to drink. The angel made it flow from the little finger of Abraham's right hand, and the baby nursed on it till he was ten days old. Then he arose, left the cave, and looked about.

*When the sun set and the stars came forth, he said,
"These are the gods!" But at dawn the stars could no
longer be seen and he said, "I will not worship these;
they are no gods." Then seeing the sun, he cried "This
is my god, him will I praise." But the sun set, and he
sighed, "He is no god." So it was also with the moon.
"This, too, is no god!" he shouted. "There is One who
sets them all in motion. Him only shall I worship."*

The hero story of David and Goliath is historical in form (if
not in fact) rather than legendary. Armed with only a sling,
Israel's hero defeats the giant Goliath, champion of the pagan
Philistines. Surely a sign of his greatness and God's blessing!

In contrast, some world-defending stories focus upon key
events in the Great Story in order to establish them as revelatory
moments. One often finds legendary elements added to the
historical record to prove that these moments were not ordinary.
We can actually trace this dramatic heightening in the Exodus
narrative. At this point I shall assume agreements in biblical
scholarship concerning the different sources found in the Exodus material. For our immediate purposes, what is of interest is
not the detail of theory but the question of story types and
functions.

Exodus 15 is generally accepted as the oldest account, of
which I shall quote only portions.

*I will sing to the Lord, for he has triumphed gloriously;
horse and rider he has thrown into the sea.... Pharaoh's
chariots and his army he cast into the sea; his picked
officers were sunk in the Red Sea. The floods covered
them, they went down into the depths like a stone....
At the blast of your nostrils the waters piled up, the*

floods stood up in a heap.... You blew with your wind,
the sea covered them; they sank like lead in the mighty
waters. Who is like you, O Lord, among the gods?
Who is like you, majestic in holiness, awesome in
splendor, doing wonders? (NRSV).

The story is about God as saviour; neither Moses nor the Israelites are mentioned. God uses the sea to vanquish Pharaoh and his army. The references to the blast of God's anger and the wind suggest that a storm destroyed the Egyptians, possibly throwing them from boats. To be sure, the phrase, "the floods stood up in a heap," has been interpreted as a reference to the dividing of the waters, though it could equally be a description of mountainous waves. This second interpretation is supported by the absence of any reference to the Israelites. Thus the first account of the Red Sea incident seems to depict a natural event, a storm that overcomes the Egyptians and enables the Hebrews to escape.

The next version of the Exodus narrative forms part of Exodus 14. God remains the central figure, but the story has been expanded to include the flight of the Israelites. We find them trapped between the sea and the forces of Pharaoh. Moses calls upon his people to witness God's mighty act. Initially, the pillar of cloud, the symbol of the divine presence, moves between the Egyptians and the Israelites, preventing any attack. Then during the night, a wind arises, driving the waters back from the shore. One pictures a shallow, marshy area where, during a storm, the edge of the sea could literally be driven back. In their panic, the Egyptians flee into the swamp thus created. The wind dies, the waters return, and they drown. The Israelites are not said to have crossed the sea; they are only observers of God's power. Seeing the Egyptians lying dead on the shore, they put their trust in the Lord.

The final version of the Exodus narrative, also in chapter 14, expands the original account with material from two additional sources. The miraculous character of the event is greatly heightened. While the power is still attributed to God, Moses becomes his agent. He stretches his hand over the waters, which divide and pile up as walls to the right and to the left. The Israelites pass through the sea on this highway. Pharaoh's army is destroyed when Moses again raises his hand, allowing the waters to collapse upon them.

Here is the full text from Exodus 14. When we read only the unemphasized portions, we have the initial, "natural" version. Read in its entirety, we have the more spectacular account.

> *Then Moses stretched out his hand over the sea.* The Lord drove the sea back by a strong east wind all night, and turned the sea into dry land; *and the waters were divided. The Israelites went into the sea on dry ground, the waters forming a wall for them on their right and on their left. The Egyptians pursued, and went into the sea after them, all of Pharaoh's horses, chariots, and chariot drivers.* At the morning watch the Lord in the pillar of fire and cloud looked down upon the Egyptian army, and threw the Egyptian army into panic. *He clogged their chariot wheels so that they turned with difficulty.* The Egyptians said, "Let us flee from the Israelites, for the Lord is fighting for them against Egypt." *Then the Lord said to Moses, "Stretch out your hand over the sea, so that the water may come back upon the Egyptians, upon their chariots and chariot drivers." So Moses stretched out his hand over the sea, and at* dawn the water returned to its normal depth. As

the Egyptians fled before it, the Lord tossed the Egyptians into the sea. *The water returned and covered the chariots and the chariot drivers, the entire army of Pharaoh that had followed them into the sea; not one of them remained. But the Israelites walked on dry ground through the sea, the waters forming a wall for them on their right and on their left.* Thus the Lord saved Israel that day from the Egyptians; and Israel saw the Egyptians dead on the seashore. Israel saw the great work that the Lord did against the Egyptians. So the people feared the Lord and believed in the Lord and in his servant Moses.

With the passage of time, the dramatic character of the Red Sea incident has been heightened to defend, against all counter-claims, the centrality of that moment. The miraculous pathway through the sea is not, however, essential to the story. As we saw, it does not appear in the earliest versions. The crucial point is that, whatever happened, it disclosed God's saving power.

World-Illustrating Stories

Like world-defending stories, world-illustrating stories assume the faith's vision of reality. They recount events taking place in that world.

Some present stories of faith's superstars, men and women whose lives depict what it is to be truly and creatively Hindu, Buddhist, Christian, or Jewish. Whether or not they speak of saints, all religious traditions have these ideal and inspiring figures; Mother Theresa, Martin Luther King, and Gandhi number among our twentieth-century religious heroes. Numerous accounts cluster about such persons, serving as vignettes of holy living. Some have a legendary character, not in this case to support the claims of the hero, but to present a more dramatic illustration of exemplary living.

A prominent virtue of such saints is their religious devotion. In Christian tradition, Satan at times employs extreme measures to disrupt their prayers. *The Little Flowers of St. Francis* tells the following tale.

> *While his companions slept, St. Francis was at prayer. Suddenly a horde of the fiercest devils burst in with a great clamour and attacked him. One took hold of him here, another there. One pulled this way, another that. Some threatened; others scolded him. And so they strove in diverse ways to disrupt his prayers.*
>
> *Then the devils seized him with yet greater fury, dragging him around the church. But St. Francis only cried the louder: "My Lord Jesus Christ, I thank You for the great love and charity that You are showing me. You but punish your servant for all his faults in this world, that he not be punished for them in the next. I accept with joy every pain and every adversity that You, my Lord, send me."*
>
> *Having been humiliated and defeated by his endurance, the devils went away.*

Within the Hindu and Buddhist faiths, a ruler is responsible for the care of his subjects. The following tale refers to a previous incarnation of the Buddha, in animal form. Even in that life, he was exemplary.

The future Buddha once lived as a golden stag who was king over a herd of five hundred deer. The king of Banaras kept the herd in a royal preserve, and each day he would send his butcher to shoot one, for he was fond of venison. The choice fell at last to a pregnant doe who pleaded for her life on the grounds that two lives were involved. Though he had been granted immunity by the king, the stag-Buddha agreed to take her place.

When informed of this, the king at once came to the park and asked the stag why, when he had been granted immunity, he was volunteering his life. The stag explained about the pregnant doe. As king of the herd, he could not ask any other deer to give its life. Thus he was prepared to die that the doe might live.

The king was overwhelmed. He had never seen such love and compassion among humans. "I am so moved by your sacrifice," he told the stag, "that I will spare both you and the doe."

"That is fine for us," said the stag, "but what of the other deer in this royal preserve?" The stag-Buddha continued until the king had promised immunity for all the creatures of the forests, birds of the air, and fish of the waters.

Finally, I offer a tale from the Hasidic tradition of Judaism. Its founder, the Baal Shem Tov, was a model of compassion.

After the death of the Baal Shem Tov, his work was taken up by his disciples. Each young rabbi would travel to the villages, telling stories of their master, reminding the people of his teachings and carrying out various duties, such as the slaying of the animals to provide kosher meat.

Whenever one young rabbi came to a certain village, he would repeat the stories, say the prayers, follow the ritual, and kill the animals. Each time he noticed a man standing at the back of the crowd who would simply shake his head. At first he dismissed him as a Gentile who rejected the ways of Israel. Then he learned that the man was in fact a leader in the synagogue and perhaps the most devout Jew in the town.

When he could stand it no longer, the rabbi spoke to the man, demanding, "Why do you shake your head? Have I not said the prayers? Have I not sharpened the knife on the whetstone to the highest keenness to reduce as much as possible the pain of the animals? What then is lacking?" The old man replied, "When the Baal Shem Tov would sharpen the knife, he moistened the stone with his tears."

Some stories of virtuous living are acknowledged to be pure fiction. Dickens' *Christmas Carol* is a Christian classic, with long-suffering Tiny Tim and a transformed Scrooge. With such narratives, however, we move closer to a second group of world-illustrating stories, those told to exemplify the religious significance of ordinary life.

During the Middle Ages, the basic issue for Christians was sin and guilt, with the host of heaven and the forces of hell contending for souls. Here is an Irish tale, with counterparts in most European cultures. I shall try to give it an Irish flavour.

There was a young man, and long ago it was, with a terrible love for card-playing and drinking the whisky.

So it was that one day he came short of money.

A man met him that night. "I often see you going home this road," said the man to him. "You can leave me be," says he; "I have no money." "Now," says the man, "I'll give you all the money you want if you will give me your note, written with your own blood, swearing that you are mine at the end of one and twenty years." It was the devil himself in the shape of a man.

He gave it to him written in his own blood that he would be his at that very time. Years later, the terrified man went to Friar Brian to seek his help. The good friar told him he would be there when the devil came for his soul.

Friar Brian came to the meeting. "What is this about? Tell me from the beginning," says Friar Brian. The devil told him that he had bought the man one and twenty years ago, and had come to claim what was his. "You may judge the case."

"Now," says Friar Brian, says he, "if you were to buy a cow or a horse at a fair, and if you gave good money in earnest for it, wouldn't you say that it was more just for you to have it than he who came only in the evening to buy?"

"Sure it is," says the devil, "the man who first paid should have it."

"Just so," says Friar Brian, "the Son of God paid earnest for this man before you bought him."

Satan had to go away then.

As we have seen, in Hinduism the Great Story of salvation and of individual hope can be inferred from the many world-illustrating stories. Complementing the tale of King Puramjana's release from the cycle of rebirth, another emphasizes the importance of the spirit of sacrifice and strict devotion to the duties of one's station in life. It both illustrates a Hindu virtue and holds out the hope of spiritual fulfilment. By satisfying the royal duty to offer protection, a king is led to the blessings of paradise.

Long ago, a beautiful dove, pursued by a hawk, sought refuge with the virtuous King Shivi. Stroking the terrified creature, the king said, "Relax little bird, don't be afraid."

At that moment, the hawk alighted beside the king. "This bird you hold was destined this day to be my food. Therefore, you should not protect him, O king. I have exerted great effort and now he must be mine. His flesh, blood, marrow, and fat will provide for my welfare and bring me great satisfaction. Therefore, O king, do not place yourself between us."

These words of the hawk troubled the king for the hawk could also claim his protection and beneficence. So the king responded, "I will order a cow or a deer to be killed and dressed for you today. Satisfy your hunger on such since I am sworn never to abandon one who seeks my protection."

The hawk replied, "O king, I do not eat such flesh as those. If you feel such sympathy, then give me your own flesh, give me of your own body, equal to the weight of this dove."

So the good king began to cut off his own flesh, balancing it against the weight of the dove. When only his skeleton remained, he ascended the scales himself, giving up his very life to keep his pledge. At once the inhabitants of the three worlds came to behold a righteous king.

Because of this self-giving act of protection, the virtuous king proceeded at once to heaven, adorned with fine jewels and riding in a golden chariot.

World-Disrupting Stories

As indicated, these stories are meant to challenge a people's faith vision, to raise doubts concerning their world-taken-for-granted. The aim is not to leave them without hope or meaning, but rather to expose the inadequacies of all religious conceptions, including all stories. In that way, they too serve faith. Being stories, however, they inevitably offer some picture of the world, some understanding of reality. And over time, they often come to be remembered more in terms of these affirmations than for their disruptive impact.

Today we read the Old Testament accounts of Ruth and Jonah, for instance, basically as world-illustrating, example stories. Ruth is seen as a model of loyalty and self-sacrifice. In its own time, however, the story would have been disturbing. The Israelites had just returned from exile in Babylon. Under the leadership of Ezra and Nehemiah, they sought to remain religiously pure. For them that meant strict separation from others in the region. Certainly intermarriage with Ammonites or Moabites was forbidden. In that context, the story of Ruth made the shocking claim that the grandmother of their hero King David was a Moabitess!

Earlier I mentioned John Dominic Crossan's assertion that the story of the Good Samaritan (for us, an example story that stresses the call to be neighbourly) would have been world-disrupting to first-century Jews. Jesus did the unthinkable when he declared the Samaritan good! He questioned the moral and religious assumptions of his contemporaries. Perhaps we can catch something of the impact of the story if we tell it again for our time. I have in mind a typical, white, middle-class congregation.

> *A young man was travelling through one of the seamier parts of a great city when he was set upon by a gang of toughs. They beat him into unconsciousness, stole his wallet and watch, and left him bleeding in an alley. By chance, a cleric was driving by and saw him, but fearful for his own safety and already late for a meeting, he drove on. Later a social worker caught sight of the youth slumped in the alley, but he excused himself, for he was a caseworker with the Children's Aid, not the John Howard Society or the Detox Centre.*
>
> *It began to grow dark. A solitary figure walked down the street. Strange place for a woman to be so late in the day! But she lived there. She was Black, and she was a lesbian. When she saw the youth, she went to him, wiped off some of the blood and dirt from his face with the edge of her skirt, and called a cab. She took him to the Good Samaritan Hospital, paying the fare with her last dollars. Which of these three proved a neighbour to the young man who fell among thieves?*

The following Sufi tale challenges the smug certitude of religious establishments. There is little danger that it will be read simply as world-illustrating!

> *One day a very traditional dervish from an austere school was strolling along a river bank, lost in thought.*

*He was startled out of his reverie by a loud shout.
From somewhere, someone was chanting the dervish
call. "That will avail nothing," he said to himself, "for
the fool is mispronouncing it. Instead of intoning YA
HU, he is saying U YA HU." Still, he thought, the
poor fellow was probably doing his best.*

*So he hired a boat and crossed over to an island in
midstream from whence he believed the sound had
come. There he found a man dressed in a dervish robe,
sitting in a reed hut. He was swaying in time to his
own chanting of the initiatory phrase. "My friend,"
said the first dervish, "you mispronounce the words.
I must tell you this, for both he who gives and he who
takes advice gain merit. The phrase must be spoken
thus, YA HU."*

"Thank you," said the other dervish humbly.

*Satisfied with himself for his good deed, the first
dervish returned to his boat. It has been written that
one who could correctly repeat the sacred formula
could even walk on water. That was something that he
had never seen, but longed one day to be able to do
himself.*

*He could hear nothing from the island as he rowed
away, but was certain that his pupil had learned the
lesson well. Soon, however, he was saddened as he
heard a halting U YA HU. The unschooled dervish
was repeating the phrase in his old way.*

*He was startled yet again by a strange sight. The
foolish dervish was walking toward him, walking on
the surface of the water.*

*Amazed, he stopped rowing. "Brother," said the
second dervish when he reached the boat, "I am sorry*

to trouble you, but I must ask again how to pronounce the chant. I find it so difficult to remember."

We have come to the end of our brief survey of the rich world of faith narratives. To be sure, religious story-tellers did not have this system in mind as they spun their yarns, nor were they confined to its classes. Often the tales they recounted do not fit neatly into my categories. In practice, our narrative types have blurred edges. Such mixed types, however, do not rule out the usefulness of our categories. They merely remind us that most religious tales are complex. Story-tellers have employed a variety of narrative types in the service of their art. The Jesus story is a case in point.

Consider stories of Jesus' miracles. I have already suggested that heroic legends are frequently recounted as world-defending stories. They are told to support the claims made for central figures in the world-defining narrative. Thus one might argue that the miracles are included to support the authority of Jesus and are not themselves world-defining. One can delete them and still affirm the basic tenets of Christianity.

Let us look at an example, the story of Jesus' power to subdue a storm.

> *One day he got into a boat with his disciples, and he said to them, "Let us cross over to the other side of the lake." So they put out, and while they were sailing he fell asleep. A windstorm swept down on the lake, and the boat was filling with water, and they were in danger. They went to him and woke him up, shouting, "Master, Master, we are perishing!" And he woke up and rebuked the wind and the raging waves; they ceased, and there was a calm. He said to them, "Where*

is your faith?" They were afraid and amazed, and said
to one another, 'Who then is this, that he commands
even the winds and the water, and they obey him?"
(Luke 8:22-25, NRSV).

Until Jesus addresses the storm, the story has the ring of
ordinary history. Then something dramatically different occurs.
We enter the realm of legend. The disciples' response of "Who
then is this, that he commands even the winds and the water,
and they obey him?" clearly indicates the world-defending
character of the tale.

What does this event claim about Jesus? The answer lies in
the Hebrew biblical tradition. The action implies more than
mere dramatic power over the forces of nature; that power is
divine. In the Genesis 1 account of creation, the waters are
divided at God's command, making a place for our world. In
one version of the Exodus, God rescues the Israelites by raising
a storm at sea, and in a later, more impressive, account, he
divides the waters (as in creation?). At still another level, the sea
represents chaos and all that opposes the divine purposes,
imagery which finds expression at many points in the Bible.
"You rule the raging of the sea; when its waves rise, you still
them. You crushed Rahab [Tiamat or Leviathan, the monster in
the Babylonian creation myth] like a carcass; you scattered your
enemies with your mighty arm" (Ps. 89:9-10). It reappears in The
Revelation of John. The beasts that fight against the people of
God rise out of the sea and, in the vision of the new heaven and
new earth, there is no more sea. God is the one whom the waters
must obey. To proclaim that Jesus commands the turbulent,
chaotic waves and they must obey is to claim that he is divine.
In the story of Jesus stilling the waters, we have mythical
allusions within a legend, which is itself inserted into a faith
biography.

A similar shift in narrative types occurs in the opening and closing chapters of the Jesus story. The full tale begins mythically, outside our space and time, with the assertion in John's prologue of the pre-existence of Christ. The language again echoes creation myths. "In the beginning was the Word.... All things came into being through him, and without him not one thing came into being" (John 1:1,3, *NRSV*). But this Creator from the time of mythical beginnings is also the central figure in a "this-worldly" biography that is about to be recounted. "And the Word became flesh and lived among us." By contrast, Mark begins his Gospel in our space and time, with the account of Jesus meeting with John the Baptist. Matthew and Luke offer birth narratives, which provide a transition from the mythical assertions in John to the purely historical events recounted in Mark. I am not claiming that Matthew and Luke had the other Gospels in mind. Indeed, while dependent upon Mark, both pre-date the Fourth Gospel. The birth narratives present moments in the full story in which the narrative type is shifting from myth to history and/or biography, from the pre-existent Christ to Jesus of Nazareth. On our narrative grid, legend lies between these. Hence, not surprisingly, we read of a miraculous virgin birth, an angelic choir, and a star guiding wise men from the East. In short, the Jesus story moves from myth to legend to history in its opening moments.

In conclusion, let me stress that in these last three chapters I am only drawing attention to the issue of narrative types and the variation in form which can occur within a single religious story. To declare a story to be myth or legend does not in itself rule out its capacity to be a powerful conveyor of religious truth. The mysteries that are the domain of faith carry us beyond the simple listing of historical facts. Religion remains "poetry plus, not science minus."

Part Four
Ah, Yes, But Which Story?

For my grandparents, society was by and large homogeneous. They knew, of course, that not everyone was Christian, but most people with whom they talked understood life in terms of the same version of the Christian story. With growing frequency, however, we now encounter folk who tell different stories. Hindus and Muslims are no longer simply people "over there" to whom we send missionaries. Literally, and via the mass media, they are now in our midst with stories we cannot ignore.

But how, then, are we to adjudicate between these conflicting claims? If religious stories offer us truth, surely we must consider this possibility for all versions of the Great Story. Which, then, is correct? Or, at least, which should we follow? How do we decide between Buddhism, Islam, Christianity, or atheism? How do we choose between Roman Catholic, Greek Orthodox, and United Church versions of the faith? Are such judgements rational in any sense, or do they simply reflect individual preferences and social conditioning? Clearly the significant role of the Great Story in our lives means that it is not enough to say, "Take your pick; they are all the same in the end." This is certainly an issue for our time, one that is personal, regional, and global.

The faithful make their truth claims in many ways. By substituting Mary and the baby for Shiva in a popular picture of the god, Indian Christians assert the divinity of Christ. Note the tilt of Mary's hip as she supports the child, a stance suggestive of the dancing Shiva. (Artist's interpretation of an eleventh-century Dancing Siva *and the later* The Mother of God.*)*

CHAPTER SEVEN

Does It Work?

More Than a Question of Truth

Religious visions are more than casual accounts of how things happen to be. The authors of Genesis 1 and 2 were not reporting that God made the heavens and the earth with the personal detachment of a chemist recording the boiling point of methanol, or an astronomer describing the many moons of Neptune. Religious claims are inevitably self-involving. Truly to have faith in a god is more than simply affirming that deity's existence; it is to risk oneself by living in terms of that conviction. In short, we are not dealing with mere ideas, but with fundamental assumptions concerning nature, human nature, and the nature of God that shape our lives and hopes. We are speaking of ideals for which people have been willing to die. In religion, truth is what one *does* as well as what one *knows*. A crucial factor, then, is the kind of life the Great Story encourages. Thus a faith vision may be true, a theological assertion may be correct, yet still be set aside (for a time, at least) because it is ineffective or has the wrong effect. A different perspective is needed; the Story must be retold or reinterpreted.

The proper telling of the Great Story then is more than a question of truth. If religion is a means of ultimate transformation, its story must be told in a way that fosters such spiritual growth. Therefore, as we tell the story, we must ask: Is it *relevant*? Is it *healing*?

Relevance

The Sufis tell a story of Moses coming upon a humble shepherd who was pouring out his love for God in prayer.

> *"O God," he cried. "I want to comb your hair and wash your clothes. O that I could kiss your hand." Moses rebuked him for this blasphemy. "God is a spirit, not some needy mortal." he growled. So he "corrected" the ignorant man. Moses was, of course, theologically correct; his assertions were "true." But later God rebuked the prophet. "Thou hast driven away one coming to Me in the only way he could comprehend. There is a gradation among men: each perceives only what at that stage he can perceive."*

Our Sufi tale raises the issue of relevance with respect to a person's intellectual ability. The theology of a Tillich or a Rahner, the religious philosophy of a Radhadkrishnan, or the spiritual insights of the great mystics, all may be true. None the less, they will be irrelevant for the many who lack the education, experience, or native intelligence to follow their thought. To be sure, intellectual power is neither a requirement for nor necessarily a sign of spiritual maturity. Indeed, relevance involves much more than being sensitive to intellectual factors; it means addressing the context of the other's life. If faith stories are world-defining and life-orienting, then it is crucial to tell them in a way that casts light upon the realities that are truly decisive for the person or community. They must be about things that really matter to people. They must be interpreted and expressed in a manner sensitive to those addressed. Albert Nolan sees this as characteristic of much in the Old Testament.

> *The message of a prophet is ... never a timeless message based upon timeless ideas. It is a particular word spoken to a particular people in a concrete situation about the meaning of their time and about what they should or should not be doing there and then.*[1]

This is not simply a matter for biblical interpretation, however. When proclaiming the faith we must always ask, "What will the folk to whom we would speak find relevant?"

Historically, Christians have given the Jesus story, told as a tale of redemption, several interpretations. Each interpretation reflects one way people have experienced the fundamental brokenness of life. For the early Church, anxiety was caused by the threat of fate, and death. Thus Holy Week spoke to them of Christ's victory over Satan and the power of death. By the Middle Ages, the focus had shifted to guilt and the fear of condemnation, as portrayed in Dante's dramatic images of hell. Folk of that day heard the Passion narrative as a story of Christ's sacrificial death to pay humanity's debt, to assuage the wrath of God, and thereby free us from condemnation. In our time, we are threatened by a sense of meaninglessness. This situation challenges the adequacy of traditional Roman Catholic and Protestant readings of the Great Story. Third-World theologians, looking at socio-economic injustice, have developed yet another reading. Chung Hyun Kyung, for example, has written:

> *Asian women theologians ... reflect on the theological meaning of the urgent issues around them such as sex-tourism. Korean women theologians call this latter part of their methodology* hyun jang *theology.*
>
> Hyun jang *is translated as the place where historical events are happening.* Hyun jang *theology evolves around the concrete issues Korean women confront in their everyday lives.*[2]

This does not mean that religious stories simply reflect the pain felt in any one community. It does mean that an effective presentation of the religious vision must establish contact with the human situation being experienced at that time by those addressed. They must be able to recognize some moment from their own life in the Story.

Some years ago, I worked for a time at a penitentiary along with other theological students. One student had just become a father. He was assigned to meet with teenage offenders serving one to three years. He spoke with great fervour of the love a father feels towards his children, comparing that to God's love. Some day, when they were fathers, he said, they would experience a father's joy as he now knew it. He was quite unaware of the fact that few of the offenders knew their fathers; often they saw only the changing consorts of their mothers, men who came home drunk and beat them. A father's love? All but one were already fathers and would talk excitedly about their kids. The student's theology concerning the fatherhood of God (leaving aside valid feminist critiques at this point) expressed orthodox Christian teaching, but the form did not fit the context. Thus it did not make contact with those addressed. They could not relate to it.

The call to take up one's cross, to work for a just society, is part of the Christian story. But for the troubled conscience that knows no rest or freedom from the frantic struggle to earn God's acceptance, it is not the needed emphasis. Similarly, Liberation Theology, which sees the human crisis in terms of poverty and economic oppression, speaks powerfully to many in Latin America. Indian Christians, however, argue that its analysis does not fit their situation, where distress is related more to caste than poverty. Many Chinese Christians also find it less than satisfactory; they believe the revolution sought by Latin Americans has already occurred, to a significant degree, in the People's Republic. For them, the immediate need is not social reform but spiritual nurture. Their theology, the way they tell the Jesus story, has to speak to that reality.

As a group, Third-World theologians have argued strenuously that relevance for marginalized persons demands a retelling of the Jesus story in a manner that addresses their situation. As Miguez Bonino puts it, "These theologians are increasingly claiming their right to 'mis-read' their teachers ... to offer their own interpretation of the theological task."[3] Chung Hyun Kyung puts it even more strongly: for the Bible to become "good news," its interpretation must be freed "from its age-old captivity by patriarchy, colonialism, and Western imperialism."[4] If the Story is to be effective, it must make contact with the context.

One can ask: Have people recognized what is truly crucial in their situation in that "relevant" telling of the Story? A telling of the faith Story that talks of the forgiveness of God and the hope of paradise may speak eloquently, but it could be told with the wrong emphasis if the crucial issues are racism, poverty, and the struggle for justice. The reverse could also be true. Relevance requires more than speaking to people in terms of what they experience as the pain and incompleteness of life; it also means bringing to their attention those aspects of life that should be focal in their understanding. So we must ask not only *what people find relevant to their situation* but also *what they ought to find relevant.* One without the other is insufficient.

Recognizing what should be focal, however, is not always easy. At the sixth assembly of the World Council of Churches in Vancouver, two perspectives were voiced. An articulate representative of First-World churches spoke of the need for Christians to devote themselves to the struggle for peace, for an end to the madness of the arms race. "I want to live," she said, "in a world where my grandchildren can survive to their eighties." She was followed by a woman from India, who pointed out, "In my country, few people reach such an advanced age." For her, the burning issue was not the threat of future war but the present reality of starvation.

This incident in Vancouver suggests one way of checking our sense of what is truly important. We can listen to what others find central. For the First-World Christian, for instance, the challenge of suffering means dealing with pain control for the cancer patient, determining limits of palliative care, or developing pastoral skills to lessen the distress and anger of grief. To the marginalized of the Third World, suffering means the agony of the Somali mother seeking food for her children, or the meaningless life of slum-dwellers in Bombay, Sao Paulo, or some northern reserve. For us, the issue of death is someone dropping dead of a heart attack, whether or not to pull the plug on life-support systems, or having enough life insurance to protect the family. For the masses of the Third World, death raises the spectre of helicopter gunships, suicides among the frustrated teens in slums, or death squads murdering human rights' workers and street kids.

Opening ourselves to hear the Jesus story recounted by women or the poor does not imply that their interpretation will be correct in every way. Affluent white males need not assume that these other interpretations are invariably superior. Nor should all First-World Christians feel guilty because they do not live in the slums of Bombay or have never been fired upon by helicopter gunships. But we do need the compassionate imagination that broadens the context of thought.

First-World Christians need the grace to move beyond their world of suffering and death, for example, in order to feel the pain and know the questions of their Third-World sisters and brothers. In his little book *On Job*, Gutierrez suggests that Job's first step in spiritual growth came when he moved beyond his own unmerited pain and suffering, placing it within the context of the unmerited suffering of the poor and oppressed of the world. Then the issue became a wholly different matter for Job. To do likewise is not to deny our pain, or to dismiss our suffering because it is so much less than that of the Somali mother or the Bosnian child. First World or Third, we face the mystery of death—our own death and the death of everyone we love. We do not brand such concerns as unworthy self-centredness, but we set all that in a larger context.

Healing Power

In discussing the impact of stories, we have noted that their power can be either creative or destructive. Consequently, when choosing a religious narrative and deciding how to tell it, one also faces the question: "Does it foster healing?"

We saw in chapter 2 that our sense of identity is profoundly shaped by the stories and heroes in our community. We are formed and transformed by those narratives that nurture our spirits. We are healed by tales that clarify our perception of reality. They hold before us heroes and ideals that nurture those things that are true, beautiful, and good. However, that vision with its accepted values and assumptions can be equally destructive. Consider those images kept alive by stories in which a people are nurtured: they can become a major obstacle, for instance, in the struggle for social reform, in the effort to bring healing to a society. For example, feminist demands for equality in Asia, Arlene D'Mello argues, are inhibited

> *because centuries of social conditioning, principally and fundamentally shaped and directed by the teachings [i.e., the stories] of the great Asian religions or by some philosophies advocating a certain way of life have made women accept their place in society both as ward of and dependent upon some man at any given stage in life.... [Thus] many of them are not only resistant to change, the idea of change may not have even crossed their minds.[5]*

Disturbing questions arise. Are the stories we tell our children conducive to creative and joyful humanness? Or do they foster a sense of fear and inadequacy, perhaps even prejudice?

These questions must be asked of all religious stories. Danger lies at the heart of the Christian story, for example, in its focus upon the Passion narrative. The crucifixion portrays suffering and death. To be a vehicle of healing, that event must become part of a story of life and hope. It has been so understood, and thus serves as a source for creative transformation, yet the primary place given to Calvary in the Jesus story has left it open to less salutary interpretations. Focusing upon a moment of death as revelatory has too often led to what Dorothee Soelle calls "theological sadism." It conjures up an image of a stern god who seems to enjoy punishing men and women. It has been known to lead to "Christian masochism," which proclaims suffering in and of itself to be good.[6]

Moreover, not only are we shaped by such stories, but we in turn shape them. In effect, as we write our story, we edit society's story, and again this can be either healing or destructive. Most people, of course, are shaped far more profoundly by society than society is by them. Feminists, for example, can do little as individuals. However, when increasing numbers of women simply refuse to accept the traditional definitions of their place in society, when, like Celie in *The Color Purple*, they tell a new story, the whole culture can be radically transformed. Thus it is important to note how the story is now being rewritten by those who inhabit a community's world-taken-for-granted. What kind of self-story is being authored?

Revelation refers to those events that become definitive for individuals or nations. These are the moments of textual revision. How such moments are integrated, the meaning they impart to the total story, is crucial. A student of mine confided that she had been the victim of a brutal sexual assault some years before. In the course of our conversation, she shared more about herself, including the fact that she had entered university on a scholarship. "Who are you?", I asked. "Are you the woman who was raped or the scholarship winner?" Smiling, she replied at once, "I am the scholarship winner." Both events were critical chapters in her life story, but how she put them together, the self-defining significance she gave to each, determined whether her story would be conducive to healing and confidence or leave her forever the helpless and fearful victim.

Life-determining events also arise for nations and communities. Elie Wiesel's *Night*, we recall, points to the horror of the death camps. In later works, Wiesel struggled to find the meaning of the Holocaust, to grapple with agonizing questions. How could so many European Gentiles close their eyes to the mass deportation of the Jews? How could the God of his Hasidic faith permit this outrage? What does it mean to be Jewish, post-Auschwitz? For some holocaust survivors, the master story now reflects a mood of cynical hopelessness that cripples all human relationships. For others, its message evokes the cry of "Never again!" and, at times, an uncritical allegiance to the state of Israel.

Wiesel's new Jewish story reveals a chastened Hebrew faith and a passionate opposition to all human suffering. Portions of that story find powerful expression in his oratorio in honour of the dead, *Ani Maamin: A Song Lost and Found Again*. What we hear is not some intellectual solution to the problem of evil, but a confession of faith and courage. The Patriarchs approach God to plead for an end to the terror. Isaac looks down at a father leading his son to the gas chamber and recalls his own story. But he had been granted a miracle. He does not understand why they are not. He is afraid even to understand, which increases the pain. Finally they leave heaven, unaware that God is going with them. They do not see the tear in God's eye. The chorus chants their belief in God despite the death camps, because of the death camps. In the face of meaningless death, they pray to God; they pray against God. But they believe. *Ani Maamin.*[7]

Who is telling the healing story for Jews today? The cynic, the Israeli patriot, or Wiesel? Each remembers what happened. In that sense, each story is true. Which one is more likely to lead to defeat, frustration, and death? Which will best orient the hearer's existence around life-giving values? Such are the questions the religious story-teller must ask.

The dropping of atomic bombs on Hiroshima and Nagasaki constituted another event of massive importance, most immediately for the Japanese, and then for the world. To be complete, all the stories of our generation must include this as a chapter. To fail to come to terms with this event, like the attempt to deny the significance of the Holocaust, amounts to an act of cowardice and denial. It makes the repetition of history more likely. How, though, does one tell the story of the mushroom clouds of August 1945 in a way that heals?

Two observations are relevant here. First, if the Holocaust and Hiroshima are to be chapters in a healing story, they must be more than chapters in the stories of the Jews and the Japanese. What does it mean to be German? What does it mean to be Christian, post-Auschwitz? What does it mean to be American in the light of Hiroshima and Nagasaki? Until these questions are faced, the full reality of these two dreadful episodes of the twentieth century will not be addressed, nor the full consequences accepted. Certainly it will not suffice to take comfort, as did Canada's prime minister, in the fact that the bombs fell on Asians rather than Europeans![8] Second, can we write a healing story using death camps or mushroom clouds as key events, or are they irredeemable symbols of death and destruction? Peter Slater insists that a religious story, to be complete, must tell of the way to salvation, to healing. Perhaps the proper place for death camps and mushroom clouds is as accounts of the power of evil, new world-illustrating stories, and not at the heart of the world-defining message. However, unless they find their place in our faith narrative, our story will not be healing.

We struggle to find the healing version of our religious stories, but in so doing, we must remember the issue of relevance. The current debate among Christians over inclusive language is an interesting case in point. For many women, the heavy male emphasis in so many traditional versions of the Christian story, coupled with the prevalent patriarchal bias and the violence against them in our culture, becomes a block to healing. Yet, for others, the Jesus story and the image of God as our heavenly father have creatively nurtured their spirits, and what they see as radical attacks upon that story are themselves experienced as destructive. Telling a healing story requires sensitivity to the other's context, even when we feel they may mis-perceive the full contextual realities. We shall return to this in the next chapter.

Yet perhaps the Great Story, correctly told, will not heal. Camus could be right. "The absurd, godless world [may be] ... peopled with men who think clearly and have ceased to hope ... [because they are caught] in a campaign in which [they are] defeated in advance."[9] Or could the ancient Aztecs have been closer to the truth with their version of the Great Story? They told of the destruction of four worlds prior to the fifth in which they lived. The tale portrayed non-beneficent, cruel gods, who "would destroy [the fifth world] if they were not amply nourished with sacrificial victims."[10] Here was a story that meant that hundreds literally had to have their hearts torn out in orgies of destruction to satisfy these gods. Could it be that the quest for a story that heals simply reflects our bias?

Medicine speaks of the placebo effect. Patients are sometimes helped significantly when given totally innocuous pills, perhaps a mere coated lump of sugar. All that is necessary is that they believe that these pills will improve their condition. Should they discover this deceit, however, the healing effects will cease, and they may be worse off than before. The analogy is clear. Is it enough to say that our religious story has a good effect upon us? What if Freud was right and religion is based upon wishful thinking? What if our potent religious tale is a spiritual placebo? How precarious a society that is based upon it! In short, the search for relevance and healing does not erase the need to confront the question of truth.

Let me share a story with you of placing things in the right context and of healing.

Once, a woman named Gotami sought help from the Buddha. "O Exalted One," she cried, "my only son is dead and I have gone to the wise, pleading for medicine to bring him back to life. All have answered that there is no such potion. 'But go,' they said, 'to the Exalted One. He may be able to help you.' Can you give me such medicine?"

The Buddha felt great compassion for Gotami. "It is well that you came to me," he said. "Go bring me some grains of mustard seed from houses in which no one has died, neither parent nor child, friend nor servant. From that I shall make this medicine."

Excited, Gotami went off to gather the grains of mustard seed. At each house she would ask for some and none refused her. "But tell me first," she would add, "has anyone died in this house?" "Oh, yes," was always the answer. A son or a daughter, a father or a wife. And she would have to go away empty-handed.

Exhausted after several days, she returned home, picked up the body of her son, and walked to the burning-ground. "My dear little boy," she sighed, "I felt as if you alone in all the world had died, but now

I see that this is the fate of all." And so saying, she placed the body on the fire.

When she returned to the Buddha, he asked, "Gotami, did you find the mustard seed for this medicine?" "No longer do I seek such," she replied. "Now I seek your teachings, O Exalted Lord."

Chapter Eight

Is It True?

I will begin with an obvious point: we cannot decide whether something is true until we know what it means. "Un perro no es un gato." Is that true? Unless I know its meaning ("A dog is not a cat"), I cannot answer that simple query. Unfortunately, decisions about religious truth claims have been made far too often without certainty of what was being said. Judging the truth of religious stories requires the clarification of their intent. What were the ancient sages asserting when they told creation narratives? What does it mean to call Jesus the Son of God? Our task is twofold: first meaning, then truth.

Meaning

The technical term for the art of discerning meaning is "hermeneutics." Such insight is normally easy in the case of spoken communication. There, speaker and listener usually share the same world, and questions for clarification can be put directly to the other party. With written texts, however, direct questioning is not possible. Indeed, the material may come from a context quite unlike our own. This can happen simply with the passage of time, as words take on new meanings. The King James Version for Psalm 119:147 reads, in part, "I prevented the dawning of the morning." That is a bizarre claim until one learns that, in seventeenth-century English, the word "prevent" means "to come before." Thus the New Revised Standard Version reads, "I rise before dawn." Complex problems can occur even with contemporary texts if they are products of a culture with radically different ideas about the natural order, for example, as in some tribal tale.

Karl Barth and Rudolf Bultmann approach the New Testament with widely different assumptions concerning the task of interpretation. Barth, in effect, denies any significant difference between the worlds of the first and twentieth centuries.

> The differences between then and now, there and here, *no doubt require careful investigation and consideration. But the purpose of such investigation can only be to demonstrate that* these differences are, in fact, purely trivial.[1]

Bultmann adopts the opposite stance. The New Testament message, he declares, is "incredible to modern man, for he is convinced that the mythical view of the world is obsolete."[2] We no longer accept a three-storied universe, with hell below and heaven above. Our twentieth-century worldview is shaped by "modern science and the modern conception of human nature as ... immune from the interference of supernatural powers."[3] In short, for Bultmann the understanding of first- and twentieth-century persons are really too dissimilar to make immediate contact. The New Testament must be translated into a form that speaks to the minds of our contemporaries. For this he looks to philosophy; in particular, existentialism as developed by Martin Heidegger.

Bultmann's position, let us note, assumes that one can retain the message of the New Testament without its form. The biblical story can be replaced by philosophy. The story of Jesus is like a fable that makes a point but can itself be discarded. Against this, I have argued that the narrative form of the gospel is a significant part of its meaning. In McLuhan's phrasing, the medium is part of the message, albeit a part which says that the meaning transcends its medium. Bultmann's position can certainly be questioned on these grounds. Yet, when considered along with Barth's, his work remains a useful reminder of the challenge of reading a text from a very different setting, of seeking to enter such a world without losing our own cultural identity, and of trying to discern its meaning for us here and now.

There are many facets to our hermeneutical task. What, for instance, is the relationship between the author's real world and the world portrayed in the story? Are we to assume that the writer of Jonah, for example, believed that a man could live three days in the belly of a great fish? Or was this the creative use of fiction, a Hebrew *Pilgrim's Progress*? Skilful narrators obviously employ a variety of literary devices to convey their message; part of the reader's task is to sort these out. When the poet says, "My love is like a red, red rose," he does not mean that the beloved has petals that fall off if she becomes too dry. Correct interpretation requires sensitivity to the creative use of language. If we fail to understand that, we compare our real world with that of the author's imaginary world, incorrectly assumed to be his or her literal view of the reality. The rejection of Genesis by Darwinists, as well as the condemnation of evolution by biblical literalists, reflects such confusion.

Imaginative literature reminds us that much discourse, including the religious, employs the poetic and metaphorical. To say, "The Lord is my shepherd," is not comparable to saying, "Mr. Jones is my banker." The latter is direct and literal. The former is a metaphor asserting that God is like a shepherd to me, although not literally a shepherd. God is and is not my shepherd.

According to Sallie McFague, the proper interpretation of metaphors depends on deciding what is and is not affirmed.[4] To say, "God is our Father," presumably implies the expectation of care and an attitude of respect; we do not, however, assume that God is our biological father. Whether this metaphor affirms or denies that God is better seen as male than female is obviously debated. Again, prior decisions on meaning are crucial.

The creative artistry of writers, of course, goes well beyond the mere use of metaphors. The New Testament, for instance, records that it is easier for a camel to go through a needle's eye than for a rich man to enter the Kingdom of Heaven. Some have attempted to "make sense" of Jesus' words by finding a gate called "the eye of the needle" or reading "rope" in place of "camel." Such "explanations" miss the use of exaggeration as a literary device. They miss the dramatic urgency of the admonition. Similarly, the differences between myth, legend, natural fiction, and history are not a matter of truth versus falsehood. They simply point to diversity in types of meaning and in the nature of truth conveyed.

Summarily, proper interpretation of texts requires being alert to a wide range of literary devices, particularly in the case of narratives and poetry. I have presented but a few.

Clearly we must reject the all-too-frequent tendency to grant cognitive validity only to language that is literally true. That position has often been justified on the grounds that it is more scientific; but modern science has long since given up the idea that its language must have a literal meaning. *Science cannot function if restricted to literal truth.* Using Reinhold Niebuhr's words, Ian Barbour asserts that most of the great scientific theories should be taken "seriously but not literally."[5] In this vein, Niels Bohr writes:

> We must be clear that, when it comes to atoms, language can be used only as in poetry. The poet, too, is not nearly so concerned with describing facts [literal accounts] as with creating images and establishing mental connections.[6]

This "poetic" character of science has not, however, diminished the confidence of scientists in the validity and importance of the whole enterprise. Most still believe they are giving us information about reality.

Let me quote Michael Goldberg, referring to the scriptures:

> One of the mistakes of fundamentalists and secularists alike is the failure to draw distinctions among different narrative genres present in the Bible, the fundamentalists accepting them all as histories and the secularists rejecting them all as myths [i.e., as fantastic fictions].[7]

The search for truth requires a more sensitive search for meaning.

Truth

In a homogeneous society, the "natural" assumption is that ours is the correct way of telling the true story. Today, that assumption is severely challenged. Sadly, too often the response to the resultant anxiety is a dogmatic siege mentality. One thinks of the Moral Majority. Or Opus Dei. Or the demands of Orthodox religious parties, which some secular Israelis call Jewish Khomeini-ism. Or Hindu fundamentalists wanting more restrictions on lower castes. Or Muslims seeking to impose strict Qur'anic moral codes on a mixed society. Religious pluralism has become more than a matter for academic discussion. It's on banners in the streets: Our Way Is the Right Way.

While the roots of religious diversity are likely obvious, it might be useful to review them. Some disparity is inevitable due to the uniqueness of individual experience. Blacks in Soweto, Aboriginal persons in the Canadian north, slum-dwellers in Sao Paulo, children reared in the comfort and security of middle-class English homes—all these will have their version of the Great Story shaped, in part, by their context.

We need not assume that any of these ways of seeing life are entirely wrong, but obviously they will be different. While perhaps not in error, they will miss important realities and values not a part of their experience, insights captured in another's tale. Moreover, as Peter Berger reminds us, these communally based views of reality usually "explain" the source of "error" in competing stories. Provocatively, he refers to such accounts as "conspiracies": "Catholicism may have a theory of Communism, but Communism returns the compliment and will produce a theory of Catholicism."[8]

The mere recognition of such conditioning, of course, does not free us from it. I may be conscious of systemic discrimination against women and certain racial groups, but that understanding will still be mine as a white male with certain unique experiences. This recognition, however, should cause us to ask whether we necessarily have it right. Because of the uniqueness of individual experience and the determining power of culture, all knowledge is relative. In Novak's words, "There is no place [for us] to stand apart from a standpoint."[9]

Where, then, lies the path towards truth? How do we escape the subjective character of our inevitably personal perceptions? The answer is that which operates in all knowing: we test it by expanding the conversation. The hope for a more adequate grasp of truth lies in a community of communities. Very young children, to a large extent, live in their own private world, filled with all sorts of fantasies. As they mature, they "learn" by testing their understandings against that of others, by seeking a shared way of perceiving the world. However, that is also the normal process for adults. If we have an experience about which we are uncertain, we compare it with the experience of others. Harré and Secord speak of "negotiating accounts," citing the example of family therapy. A husband and wife discuss their marriage with a counsellor who seeks to help them truly hear each other. They may or may not reach a common view, but, to understand each other's viewpoint, even if they may still disagree, is progress. It may even inspire them to rewrite their stories.[10]

The stories within which we live shape how we see reality. They draw attention to things we might otherwise miss; they emphasize truths and values we might otherwise forget. Yet the very fact that these stories stress some aspects of truth, some values, means that they will tend to neglect others. Metaphorically speaking, stories provide light by which we see reality but, in so doing, they also cast shadows. A powerful way to dispel those shadows, to bring neglected truths and values to our attention, is to illuminate them by the light of another story. The search for the validation of our version of the Great Story follows the path of all knowledge; we must listen to others.

A word of warning: we may not want to hear the other version. We may refuse to negotiate honestly. "We are tempted," Gutierrez warns, "to measure progress in dialogue [almost entirely] ... in terms of our own ability to get a hearing for our own viewpoint, in terms of the relative openness or resistance of our interlocutors to our point of view."[11] Too often we are keen on telling our story but not on listening while others tell theirs. Too frequently we lack the hermeneutical skill and the moral courage to risk understanding them, lest we be changed thereby. In traditional religious terms, the quest for fuller understanding demands an openness to being evangelized by the other person even as we witness to our own faith vision.

For the purposes of our discussion, I shall again focus on the Judaeo-Christian tradition. As we explore dialogue, the reader should remember that my perspective is as a white, male, middle-class, and First-World Christian. That is my starting point, and in light of what has just been said, I cannot escape that fact. My thoughts on necessary dialogues, then, will reflect that setting, although I believe they have their counterparts among those living in different contexts. In each case, our discussion will be cursory. My intention is simply to illustrate that the search for truth in an expanded conversation is already under way.

Dialogue with those telling different versions of the Christian story. Here, we can distinguish two forms of dialogue. One is the exchange taking place between members of different denominations, a dialogue between persons of relatively equal status or power. Ours has been called the age of ecumenism.

Beginning first with varieties of Protestants, the conversation has expanded. Roman Catholics are now active in the World Council of Churches, and Protestant observers formed part of Vatican II. Orthodox, Roman Catholics, and Protestants are sharing their interpretation of the Christian story, not primarily to convert others, but to deepen their own understanding and commitment through that sharing. These exchanges, largely friendly and non-contentious, have produced significant shifts in the theologies of the various churches. Protestants are finding a greater place for Mary in their Christian story, and for richer liturgies in their services. Roman Catholics are moving to a new appreciation of Luther and an emphasis upon the Bible and the laity that, at times, surpasses that of some Reformed Churches.

Yet even more significant, I believe, is the emerging exchange within Christendom in which the "voiceless" are demanding to be heard. Their stories and their perspective on the faith have largely been ignored. The marginalized, especially women, non-whites, and the poor, are challenging the "authorized version," a tale primarily told and interpreted by relatively affluent, white, older males. We shall look briefly at two of these challenges.[12]

Feminist writers have increasingly made the case that the dominant stories of Western culture generally, and of the Judaeo-Christian tradition in particular, have been told with a male bias. Consequently, they neither reflect nor relate adequately to the experience of women. Though too sophisticated to say that God is male, that tradition has primarily adopted masculine language. We are more apt to hear of the good shepherd than the good housewife, of God, the Lord of Hosts and mighty warrior, than of God, the caring, nurturing, mother figure, portrayed in Hosea 11. Such usage has clearly influenced the culture's image of women, men, and God. The story thus narrated too often becomes not only patriarchal but gynocidal. Women are pictured as evil flesh, as defective males, or as symbols of such purity that they are effectively denied their sexuality, not to mention active participation in the economic and political spheres. The result? A frightening spectrum of assaults upon women, including the tragedy of the witch hunts. (Such sadistic aggression is, of course, not confined to the West or to the Hebraic-Christian tradition.[13])

Similarly, because the Christian story as traditionally recounted says God is more like a man than a woman, the deity tends to be associated with those attributes assigned to men. *He* is portrayed as strong, dominant, even jealous, and given to rage. As a result we too often find a despotic, *macho* god. Jealously he calls for the total destruction of Jericho and everything in it. Similarly, as we have seen, God the Father is pictured as offended and full of wrath, a condition only to be assuaged by the death of the loving Son. Since God is the symbol of the highest ideal, we end with a "war-making, people-killing, and nature-destroying world."[14] In contrast, feminists argue that "women have not been known for destroying the lives of their children in order to defend their 'isms.'"[15]

Drawing upon what they see as women's experience, such writers not only raise objections to the traditional account but add new emphases. They would replace the hierarchical tendencies they find in male theology with a more egalitarian stance. To cite a frequent image, Sarah's circle replaces Jacob's ladder. Or to take one final example, their theology places a greater emphasis on creation spirituality. Women, they believe, are more attuned to nature by their very psychological and physical make-up. They are cosmocentric rather than anthropocentric in their views. Animals and plants, indeed, the whole eco-system, become important in the plan of God. These are but a few of the issues raised by a feminist rendering of the Christian story. One need not agree with every criticism to recognize the importance of hearing this other perspective.

The poor, as well as feminists, have challenged the "authorized version." How is Christian faith made relevant to five million "street kids" in Brazil, some as young as four years of age, who have been abandoned to live by their wits? How do we speak of the world-wide Christian community to slum-dwellers in Sao Paulo or Bombay? They know that most of the world's wealth is controlled by a minority, largely claiming to be Christian. All theology, I have maintained, is written from some standpoint. Speaking from an Argentine perspective, Miguez Bonino writes:

> *All we have today in Latin America are reactionary, reformist, or revolutionary engagements, and therefore reactionary, reformist, or revolutionary readings of what we have called the "germinal events of the Christian faith."*[16]

What we need now, he argues, is a revolutionary version. For these Christians, all theology begins with commitment; theirs, with what they see as God's preferential option for the poor. The story must be told from the underside of history, from the vantage point of the powerless and those without material comfort. When so recounted, it will be a very different story.

The writing of such theology will not be easy, however. It is hard for Asian women theologians, for instance, when (like so many) they have been trained in Western seminaries and have heard and reheard the "authorized version." They must turn to the marginalized in their midst and listen to their story.

*Women from various backgrounds gather and listen
to one another's stories of victimization and liberation.
Educated middle-class women theologians are
committed to inviting or visiting poor farmers, factory
workers, slum-dwellers, dowry victims and prostitutes
and listening to their life story.*[17]

The point I would make is not that these "other" Christian stories are *the true* versions, but that light is thrown on the theological scene, and new insights emerge when they are added to the conversation. Parallel situations exist today in other religious communities. Feminist criticism of the "authorized version" is occurring in Jewish circles. Religious protests on the part of the poor, tribals, and marginalized can be found in India, among Hindu as well as Christian writers, giving birth to the so-called Dalit theology. The marginalized people of various faith communities—those who are Third World in the sense of being the third person, the ones talked about but who do not speak—are all demanding the opportunity to develop their own interpretation of the faith story. They are insisting that their version be heard.

There remains one final, perhaps controversial, dimension of story sharing within the Christian community. What of the story told to us by those whose version and lifestyle we feel unable to accept? Should we listen to them or dialogue with them? Would their account of the Great Story enlighten any dark places in our interpretation or merely confuse and mislead?

The homosexual community provides a case in point. Should they be part of the ongoing Christian conversation? This, assuredly, is a matter of hot debate. Let me be clear: The issue I am raising is not the scientific debate as to whether or not they are free to choose another orientation. Nor is it judgement concerning the morality of their lifestyle. We need not agree on these matters. Rather, does a sincere quest for truth demand an openness incompatible with deciding in advance that one or more groups can be excluded from the search? Can any faction, even the majority, adequately write the definitive, Christian account of humanity's spiritual journey, while refusing to hear from a significant element within the community? More than a matter of false consciousness, more than the blindness that hardly realizes it has excluded women, Blacks, and the poor from the critical conversation, here is a conscious decision that some are not worthy to participate. Yet surely creativity lies in the power of dialogue, not in prejudging other persons' views or their immediate relevance for our situation. Insight comes through exchanges with others that clarify our perspective as together we search for truth.

Dialogue with those telling a different faith story. The recognition that dialogue does not presume agreement, either before or after the discussion, is obviously an assumption operative in all interfaith exchanges. Yet if such conversations are to be honest, the participants must also accept the risk of their being changed, even converted.[18] Asian and African Christians have little option, for their life is set amidst powerful expressions of other faiths.

In Africa one must differentiate between the mainly Black south and the Arab north. In the latter situation, Christians form a minority facing a Muslim majority. Their context for dialogue is akin to Asian encounters with Hinduism or Buddhism. For the moment, let us look at the Black south where Christians, if not a majority, often form a significant minority. Largely European and North American interpretations of the faith have dominated the way the Christian story has been told there. This "authorized version" was presumed to contain all that was necessary and only required translation into a form that Africans could understand. White Christians seemingly had nothing to learn from Blacks, Christian or non-Christian. Transformations in the story were limited to a few "native" touches such as drums in the liturgy. However, the emergence of Black consciousness among Africans has forced Europeans to consider the need for new ways to tell the Jesus story. Some, for instance, have sought to relate the strong African emphasis upon spirits, especially the spirits of ancestors, to what Christians mean by the Holy Spirit and the communion of saints. Such exchanges could end in nothing more than the domestication of African religious experience, but they could also be occasions for reformulating the vision of faith. Again, it is a matter of honesty in the quest for truth.[19]

In Asia, as in Africa, religious history is marred by cultural and racial imperialism. Christianity came as a white and Western import. In Asia, however, Christians encounter indigenous cultures powerfully shaped by sophisticated, articulate, and well-organized faiths. Hinduism, Buddhism, Islam, Confucianism, and Shinto are traditions with long recorded histories. Here the challenge is particularly urgent. C. S. Song accuses Christians of practicing "spiritual apartheid," acting as if they had been given monopoly rights to salvation. They must learn, he argues, to listen while Muslims and Buddhists tell their story, and open themselves to the possibility of being changed by the encounter. They will not necessarily cease to be Christians, yet in honest dialogue the risk is always there.

Among Asian Christian women who share in the feminist struggle against patriarchal and oppressive religion, one finds a growing awareness of this need to be open to those of other faiths and to search out the feminine images of God in the traditional religions.[20] For them, this requires being open not merely to the so-called great world religions but also to tribal and even "primitive" forms.

> *More recently Asian women are drawing strength from the popular religions of the people. These ancient religious traditions are the religions of the poor and marginalized. They often contain within them elements of protest which can become a force for social change.... Asian women recognize that religiousness can become oppressive and escapist, but there is a realization that these traditional popular religions cannot be ignored— they have to be appropriated to become a force in the transformation of society.*[21]

Christian-Marxist dialogue is yet another encounter of at least a quasi-interfaith character.[22] The character of that dialogue has been strongly influenced by the diverse, societal contexts in which it has occurred. Christians from Eastern Europe (before 1989), the People's Republic of China, Latin America, as well as Western Europe and North America, all living in quite distinct contexts, have spawned different styles of discussion. In each, however, creative encounters have occurred, affecting the way the Christian story has been told.

Summarily, religious visions, versions of the Great Story as articulated by various faith communities, are being challenged in our ever-more complex and pluralistic world. One response has been a retreat into dogmatic fundamentalism. Another, and, I suggest, a more creative one, carries such visions into an open exchange with others. Here, in the mutual sharing of stories, believers seek clarification, if not consensual validation, in an ever-expanding conversation. Those who will not listen will never know even the truth of their own faith.

Five blind men came upon something quite new to them. "It is an elephant," said its young attendant. Reaching out, the tallest of the men took hold of the elephant's ear. "I have a large and rather tough leaf," he announced. "Indeed it is a tree," concluded the shortest man, "for I have found the trunk." As he spoke he ran his hands up and down one of the elephant"s legs. "Nonsense! cried a third man who had just bumped into the elephant's side. "It is some kind of a wall, perhaps part of a holy temple." "Then where does this rope fit in?" queried the fourth man whose hands grasped the tail. At that moment the elephant wrapped its trunk around the last man. "I am lost!" he cried. "It is in fact a python."

Part Five:
A Personal Testimony

The great theologian was struggling to complete another of his magnificent tomes. Feeling the need for solitude, he hired a humble believer to row him across the lake to a secluded spot.

Making idle conversation, he asked, "Have you read any of these books?"

The poor man stopped long enough to mutter, "Can't read."

"You are illiterate," said the great scholar. "Half of your life has been wasted."

Halfway across the lake, a violent storm erupted, and the boat began to take water. The rower looked intently at his passenger. "Have you learned to swim?"

"No time for such," was the stern response.

"Then all of your life is lost, for we are sinking."

Who grasps the truth?

A man once said to his double-seeing son, "Son, you see two instead of one."

"How can that be, Father?" the boy answered. "If I did, there would seem to be four moons in place of two."

CHAPTER NINE

The Poison Arrow, the Ringing Bell

What can I say to you now, as we near the end of our journey through the stories of faith? Let me propose three elements for your reflection.

God-talk, be it stories or theology, exists to nurture faith. Religion is, first of all, a way of life that offers hope for ultimate transformation. Christianity is primarily a matter of individual and communal life, guided by the example of Jesus of Nazareth and empowered by the Holy Spirit. It orients the faithful towards the promise expressed in such images as eternal life, the Kingdom of God, even a new heaven and a new earth. God-talk must always be secondary to, and the servant of, that way of life. Liberation theologians reflect this understanding when they call theology the second act, following the first act, commitment.

> *Theology, as here conceived, is not an effort to give a correct understanding of God's attributes or actions*

but an effort to articulate the action of faith, the shape of praxis conceived and realized in obedience.... Orthopraxis, *rather than orthodoxy, becomes the criterion for theology.*[1]

In a radically different context, Aarne Siirala, a theologian with strong interests in the field of psychotherapy, laments that theologians have often been preoccupied with their conceptual systems rather than the saving realities of the faith. "There has to be a funeral for many problems of the classical theological tradition if theology wants to be a participant in articulating the language of healing and transformation."[2]

No theology can capture the truth. The image of religion emerging here sounds a warning call against all theological pretensions. Barth described himself as once having been like a man stumbling in the darkness of a church tower. He reached out desperately and grabbed a rope to steady himself, only to find that he had rung the great bell. Thus he described his experience of discovering the point of entry for his theological reflections. One wonders whether some theologians think that they have also turned on the light and dispelled all darkness, as if they can now see clearly.

Barth's image, assuredly, is apt in pointing to the revelatory experience, that self- and world-defining moment that reorients our being. But we must never forget that while the insights so derived may be true, they are not the truth. To use Alves' words, theologians are not permitted to speak the truth, but only to contemplate the horizons of eternity. The tendency to religious or theological pride is not peculiar to theologians, however. We are all tempted to seek spiritual security by claiming absoluteness or infallibility for our faith understanding. And whether the god-talk be of a sophisticated, theological system or the homey truths and stories learned as children, we too easily forget that at best we witness to ultimate mysteries. So Alves calls us to remember both "the truth of heresy" and "the heresy of truth."[3]

To speak of the *truth of heresy* is to remember that our experience of God is not the only valid encounter with the divine. As we have seen, the quest for religious truth requires being open to the possibility of genuine spiritual insights even in the thought and experience of those with whom we disagree. We must be prepared to learn from followers of other traditions (even atheists) or from Christians in other denominations whose understanding of the faith is seriously at odds with our own.

Beyond that, the conversation must be expanded to include those whose lived experience is different and who are often ignored in the articulation of faith. The "marginalized"—women, the poor, Blacks, and probably groups yet unrecognized—must be allowed to "correct" us. Such sensitivity does not imply that these become the standards of religious truth or that we have betrayed our own experience of God; it merely recognizes that the Holy Spirit is not confined within the perimeter of the community that thinks as we do.

Clearly, what I have just said reflects my own situation as a white male in an affluent society. It is the challenge that I personally face, and more than this, it mirrors theological reality. The vast majority of traditional theology has been written by white males in affluent societies who too often paid little attention to the stories of women, the poor, and non-whites. This situation, however, merely exemplifies a broader issue. Men of whatever race or economic status must learn to listen to women. White women as well as white men must pay heed to non-whites, and the rich, whatever their colour or sex, to the poor.

Let me change the context. For Chung, as an Asian woman,

Christocentrism (which had such an important and creative place in Barth's theology) must be challenged. Too often it has led to bigotry, which blocks transformation by the religious wisdom of other faiths, including, in her thought, tribal religions and shamanism. "To recognize the plurality in diverse manifestations of the divine," she writes, "is important in order to fight the fascist, imperialistic mentality that fosters exclusivity of one's own claim to truth."[4] No wonder her words caused such a strong reaction at the seventh assembly of the World Council of Churches in Canberra!

To speak of the *heresy of truth* is to remember that god-talk, at best, points to a mystery that always eludes it. Religion is "poetry plus." In Tillich's phrase, God is always beyond God. Story is a preferred medium for religious discourse precisely because it challenges the adequacy of its proclamation. It declares that the message inevitably transcends the capacities of the medium, the power of both story-teller and story. Theologians must remain keenly aware that they offer but a fallible witness to the truth.

Douglas John Hall points to aspects of our contemporary situation that heighten this need for intellectual humility. Christians, as a total community, are increasingly marginalized in a pluralistic world. The power and influence once exercised by a triumphant Church is fast fading, and we are being forced to admit the possibility of truth in other traditions. Our challenge is to avoid the siege mentality and arrogant dogmatism that is the defence of the fearful. Hall puts it this way:

> *The invitation to discipleship that is extended to us in this historical moment is precisely an invitation, and indeed a command, to rid ourselves once and for all of these "pretensions of finality" (Reinhold Niebuhr) ...*

> *to exchange our inheritance of theological triumph for*
> *the modesty that Karl Barth rightly says inheres in*
> *this most modest science, Christian theology....*[5]

Following its centuries of dominance, at least in the West, the present crisis in the Church will perhaps occasion the recognition of what has always been true: we live, in Reinhold Niebuhr's words, as those having, yet not having, the truth.[6] Few, one assumes, would dispute this, but the writings of many Christians, including theologians, frequently fail to evoke such attitudes.

One final note: Theological "pretensions to finality" have other serious consequences. They mean more than a failure to formulate our ideas properly. Religion, as we have said repeatedly, is a vehicle for ultimate transformation. If it is to be effective, if it is to nurture others in that revolutionary relationship that we call the grace of God, then, as I have suggested, our witness must encourage women and men to venture beyond their personal and communal religious systems. Their trust must not be in their theology, however well articulated, nor even in the stories of faith, however powerful, but in God. Only thus will our god-talk truly serve the faith.

Faith is a risk. Have we then reached the end of our journey? Through dialogue, through sharing our stories, do we arrive at the truth? Or would such confidence be misplaced and contrary to the nature of faith? Paul Tillich proposed a three-fold relationship between faith and doubt. Two are positive, one negative. I would add a second negative form.

Doubt in the form of *skepticism* is contrary to faith. Perhaps more precisely, it is a competing faith, a synoptic vision that questions the meaningfulness of life. Often it pictures a universe indifferent to the hopes and fears of humanity. It invites another dialogue for religious persons, one with atheism. Tillich believed that, expressed in Stoicism, it is the primary viable alternative to biblical faith for most Westerners.

I see a second negative form, which might be called *immoral doubt*. Faith entails obedience. Religion, I have argued, pertains to those images, heroes, and goals that are life-orienting. Tillich speaks of our ultimate concern demanding total surrender[7] and Baillie of the holy as what I would rather die than betray.[8] Thus, I suggest, we must recognize the potential for a form of doubt that reflects a failure of courage.

Robert McAfee Brown asserts that sometimes "we doubt because we fear that our faith is true."[9] We doubt because we are unwilling to face the moral implications of belief. Similarly Baillie writes, "Part of the reason why I could not find God was that there is that in God which I did not wish to find."[10] Admittedly, these are Christian theologians. I do not cite them, however, as proving the existence of God, let alone the Christian understanding. Religion carries an imperative; its truth is not simply to be believed but also to be acted upon. Reluctance to obey that imperative could be concealed by arguing that the faith is cognitively untenable. Alternatively, it could be modified, for example, in defence of racist assumptions. Recognizing the possibility of such error, we must always be cautious in making claims for our particular faith vision.

The word "God" points to a mystery transcending all conceptualizations. To forget this is to seek security in our own cleverness, in our theology rather than in God, however envisaged. It is to be tempted by intellectual pride. The history of religious wars stands as a sad reminder of the consequences of forgetting this. The first of Tillich's positive forms, *methodological doubt*, points to openness, a readiness to modify one's religious conceptions, to recognize their "essential revisability."

Tillich also posited a final creative relationship, which he called *existential doubt*. This is the uncertainty that comes with the awareness that faith is finally beyond absolute proof, because it pertains to those basic convictions upon which all other thinking rests. Faith thus entails risk, committing one's self to what is believed or experienced to be ultimate truth and goodness, that for which one would die. Yet it cannot be proven true beyond all doubt.

Faith, to be true to its own nature, must include the acceptance of such insecurity. We could be wrong. Perhaps there is no power of goodness at the heart of reality; possibly Jesus was simply confused, the Buddha mistaken, Mohammed misguided. Though the idea carries no conviction for me, perchance the Aztecs were right. Our world may be the product of cruel gods who demand bloody sacrifice, sacrifice we express today in the madness of war. Living faith must have the courage to absorb such doubt.

Tillich draws the analogy with heroism. The courageous soldier is not one without fear. The latter would not be brave, simply naive or stupid, for the dangers are real. The truly brave are those who go on in spite of fear. Similarly, "the doubt which is implied in faith accepts this insecurity in every existential truth ... and takes it into itself in an act of courage."[11] Faith is the courage to affirm, to risk commitment. There is no option. The agnostic who says, "I will take no stand until all is certain," has made a commitment to that stance. We seek ultimate truth but can never be sure we have found it. We are destined to live by faith, not by sight. By sharing our stories, we can exercise that courage in a quest for enlightenment with others who also seek the truth.

The Buddha told this story. A certain man was wounded by a poison arrow, but he would not allow the surgeon to treat him until he learned the name and caste of the man who sought his life. He demanded to know the poison and the type of string in the bow, the wood in the arrow's shaft, and the feathers affixed to its end. "That man will die with his questions unanswered," said the Lord Buddha. "So it is with everyone who says, 'I will not follow the holy life, I will not venture in faith, until all my religious doubts are overcome, and I have a full theology.'"

Notes

Part One

Chapter 1   Story-tellers, One and All

1. Eric Berne, *Transactional Analysis in Psychotherapy* (New York: Grove Press, 1961), *passim*. Berne suggested that we operate in what he called three "ego states," Parent, Adult, and Child.
2. John Baillie, *Our Knowledge of God* (New York: Charles Scribner's Sons, 1959), 244.
3. Joseph C. McLelland, *The Clown and the Crocodile* (Richmond, Virginia: The John Knox Press, 1970), *passim*.
4. The festivals are sketched in such works as Alan Unterman, *Jews: Their Religious Beliefs and Practices* (London: Routledge & Kegan Paul, 1981).
5. Scholars tend to use the neutral designations B.C.E. (Before the Common Era) and C.E. (Common Era), rather than B.C. (Before Christ) and A.D. (Anno Domini or Year of the Lord) to avoid what could be seen as Christian imperialism.
6. Details of the Hajj can be found in such works as David E. Long, *The Hajj Today* (Albany, N.Y.: State University of New York Press, 1979). Muhammad Abdul-Rauf, "Pilgrimage to Mecca," *National Geographic* (Nov. 1978), provides an excellent illustrated discussion.

Part Two

Chapter 2   To Remind Us Who We Are

1. Sam Keen, *To a Dancing God* (New York: Harper & Row, 1970), 101.
2. H. Richard Niebuhr, *The Meaning of Revelation* (New York: The Macmillan Company, 1941). At times Niebuhr speaks of inner rather than internal history.
3. Alfred Adler, *What Life Should Mean to You* (New York: Capricorn Books, 1958), 19.
4. In a time when we read much about the sexual abuse of children, often reported long after the incident, one realizes that it is important to discern, for both the alleged victim and the victimizer, whether or not the memory is to be trusted. None the less, Adler's point remains. The way the individual remembers, be that accurate or not, shapes her or his identity.
5. Wilfrid Cantwell Smith, *Towards a World Theology* (Philadelphia: Westminster Press, 1981), 7.

6. Elizabeth Stone, *Black Sheep and Kissing Cousins: How Our Family Stories Shape Us* (Penguin Books, 1989).
7. Niebuhr, *The Meaning of Revelation*, 60-61 (emphasis mine).
8. See for example Peter Berger, *Invitation to Sociology* (New York: Anchor Books, 1963), chap. 5.
9. Alice Walker, *The Colour Purple* (New York: Pocket Books, 1985), 213.
10. Walker, *The Colour Purple*, 42.
11. Walker, *The Colour Purple*, 207.
12. Among other places see Paul Tillich, *Dynamics of Faith* (New York: Harper & Row, 1957), chap. 1.
13. Mahatma Gandhi, quoted in Erik Erikson, *Gandhi's Truth* (New York: W.W. Norton & Co., 1969), 124.
14. Elie Wiesel, *Night* (New York: Avon Books, Discus Edition, 1969), 44.
15. This, I would stress, is an anthropological account of revelation that neither invokes nor necessitates the concept of a personal, self-revealing deity. It is not, however, incompatible with theological accounts. William Temple, for example, speaks of revelation as the "intercourse of mind and event," a process that brings together an external event, be that spectacular or routine, and a mind moved to "appreciate" that event's deeper meaning, in our terms, an event in external history that came alive as internal history (William Temple, *Nature, Man and God*, [London: Macmillan & Co., 1934], 315f). This is revelation from a human perspective. Theists merely assert the presence of God in both event and act of appreciation.
16. In *Dawn* and *Beggar in Jerusalem*, Wiesel explores what it means today to be Jewish. In *The Town Beyond the Wall*, he examines how the population of Europe could close its eyes to what was happening.
17. Walker, *The Colour Purple*, 214.

Chapter 3   When Stories Happen to Us

1. Gabriel Marcel, *The Mystery of Being* (London: The Harvill Press Ltd., 1950), 211ff.
2. Cf. such works as Ian G. Barbour, *Issues in Science and Religion* (Englewood Cliffs, New Jersey: Prentice-Hall, 1966); John Dillenberger, *Protestant Thought and Natural Science* (Garden City, New York: Doubleday & Co., 1960); Richard S. Westfall, *Science and Religion in Seventeenth-Century England* (New Haven: Yale University Press, 1958); Giorgio de Santillana, *The Crime of Galileo* (Chicago: The University of Chicago Press, 1955).
3. Steven Weinberg, *The First Three Minutes* (New York: Basic Books, 1977).
4. Wilfred C. Smith, "The True Meaning of Scripture: An Empirical Historian's Nonreductionist Interpretation of the Qur'an," *International Journal of Middle East Studies*, 11 (1980), 487.

5. Urban T. Holmes, *Ministry and Imagination* (New York: The Seabury Press, 1981), 151.

6. Rubem Alves, *La Teología Como Juego* (Argentina: Ediciones la Aurora, 1982), 72, 89 (translations mine).

7. John Dominic Crossan, *The Dark Interval* (Niles, Illinois: Argus Communications, 1975), 105-06 (emphasis his).

8. John C. Hoffman, *Law, Freedom and Story* (Waterloo, Ont.: Wilfrid Laurier University Press, 1986), 36.

9. Crossan, *The Dark Interval*, 77, 121, 122.

10. Idries Shah, *The Way of the Sufi* (Penguin Books, 1974), 250.

11. Eric Berne, *Beyond Games and Scripts* (New York: Grove Press, 1976), 128.

12. John Grinder and Richard Bandler, *The Structure of Magic*, vol. 2 (Palo Alto: Science and Behavior Books, 1976), 3.

13. Joanne Bernstein, "Helping Young Children to Cope with Acute Grief: A Bibliotherapy Approach," in Vanderlyn R. Pine et al., eds., *Acute Grief and the Funeral* (Springfield, Ill.: C. C. Thomas Publishers, 1976), 274.

14. Dylan Thomas, "Notes on the Art of Poetry," in *20th Century Poetry and Poetics*, Gary Geddes, ed. (Toronto: Oxford University Press, 1969), 554.

15. Of course, the creative transformation of a nation through the overcoming of social injustice requires changing unjust social structures, bad laws, unequal economic and educational resources, as well as changing the way people think. Creative change has both subjective and objective dimensions. But objective change, unaccompanied by subjective modification, is unlikely to last, just as subjective change, transformation of self-consciousness, that does not lead to objective transformations of the social structure proves empty, if not hypocritical.

16. Celia Coates, "Once upon a Session: Healing Stories and the Re-enchantment of Psychotherapy," *Common Boundary* (Jan.-Feb. 1990), 12-16.

17. Ira Progoff, *The Symbolic and the Real* (New York: Julian Press, 1963), 78.

18. Augusta Jellinek, "Spontaneous Imagery," *American Journal of Psychotherapy* 3 (1949), 380.

19. O. Carl Simonton et al., *Getting Well Again* (Los Angeles: J. P. Tarcher, 1978), *passim*.

20. D. W. Winnicott, *Playing and Reality* (London: Tavistock Publications, 1971), 54.

21. Progoff, *The Symbolic and the Real*, 122.

22. Peter Berger, *The Sacred Canopy* (Garden City, New York Doubleday, 1967), *passim*.

23. Turner and Turner, *Image and Pilgrimage in Christian Culture*, 250.

24. Winnicott, *Playing and Reality*, 54.

25. K. H. Ting attributes this to W. H. Auden in an article, "Theological Mass Movements in China," *Chinese Theological Review* (1985), 69. I have not been able to find it in Auden.

Part Three

Chapter 4   What Goes Where?

1. Hugh Kenner in John Dominic Crossan, *In Parables* (New York: Harper & Row, 1973), 2.
2. One needs be careful here. Some authors use the term myth to mean what I have called world-defining stories. This confusion easily arises from the fact that many important myths, such as creation narratives, in fact function as key portions of world-defining story. However, not all portions of that story are myths. Hence it is best to use terms which distinguish between world-definition and other-worldly settings.

Part Four

Chapter 7   Does It Work?

1. Albert Nolan, *Jesus before Christianity* (Maryknoll, New York: Orbis Books, 1978), 76.
2. Chung Hyun Kyung, *Struggle to be the Sun Again* (Maryknoll, New York: Orbis Books, 1990), 107.
3. Jose Miguez Bonino, *Doing Theology in a Revolutionary Situation* (Philadelphia: Fortress Press, 1975), 62.
4. Chung Hyun Kyung, *Struggle to be the Sun Again*, 107.
5. Arlene D'Mello, "Image, Status and Reality of Asian Women in Asia and in Australia," in *In God's Image* (December 1989), 19, 21.
6. Dorothee Soelle, *Suffering* (Philadelphia: Fortress Press, 1975), 9-32.
7. Elie Wiesel, *Ani Maamin, A Song Lost and Found Again* (New York: Random House, 1973), 19, 43, 105.
8. The Diaries of William Lyon Mackenzie King for August 1945 (Public Archives of Canada) as reported in Peter Slater, *The Dynamics of Religion* (San Francisco: Harper & Row, 1978), chap. 9.
9. Albert Camus, *The Myth of Sisyphus* (New York: Vintage Books, 1959), 68-9.
10. Nigel Davies, *The Aztecs: A History* (London: Macmillan Co. Ltd., 1973), 145.

Chapter 8   Is It True?

1. Karl Barth, *The Epistle to the Romans* (London: Oxford University Press, 1968), 1 (emphasis mine).

2. Rudolf Bultmann, *Kerygma and Myth* (New York: Harper Torchbooks, 1961), 3.
3. Bultmann, *Kerygma and Myth*, 7.
4. Sallie McFague, *Speaking in Parables* (Philadelphia: Fortress Press, 1975) and *Metaphorical Theology* (Philadelphia: Fortress Press, 1982).
5. Ian G. Barbour, *Myths, Models and Paradigms* (New York: Harper & Row, 1974), 7.
6. Quoted in Werner Heisenberg, *Physics and Beyond* (New York: Harper Torchbooks, 1972), 41.
7. Michael Goldberg, *Theology and Narrative* (Nashville: Abingdon, 1982), 204.
8. Peter Berger, *Invitation to Sociology*, 51.
9. Michael Novak, *Ascent of the Mountain, Flight of the Dove*, 62.
10. R. Harré and P. F. Secord, *The Explanation of Social Behaviour* (Oxford: Basil Blackwell, 1972) 236.
11. Gustavo Gutierrez, "Reflections from a Latin American Perspective: Finding Our Way to Talk about God," in Virginia Fabella and Sergio Torres, eds. *Irruption of the Third World* (Maryknoll, N.Y.: Orbis Books, 1983), 230.
12. Among feminist works are included: Rosemary R. Ruether, *Religion and Sexism* (New York: Simon & Schuster, 1974) and *Sexism and God-talk* (Boston: Beacon Press, 1983); Letty M. Russell, *Human Liberation in a Feminist Perspective* (Philadelphia: Westminster Press, 1974); Phyllis Trible, *Texts of Terror: Literary Feminist Readings of the Bible* (Philadelphia: Fortress Press, 1984); Elizabeth Fiorenza, *In Memory of Her* (New York: Crossroad, 1983); Jacquelyn Grant, *White Women's Christ and Black Women's Jesus* (Atlanta, Georgia: Scholars Press, 1989). Ms. Grant offers a strong critique of most feminist theology as narrowly white. Chung Hyun Kyung, *Struggle to be the Sun Again*, feminist theology from an Asian perspective.

   Among Black theological works are included: James H. Cone, *Black Theology and Black Power* (New York: Seabury Press, 1969) and *A Black Theology of Liberation* (Maryknoll, N.Y.: Orbis Books, 1986); C. Eric Lincoln, *Race, Religion and the Continuing American Dilemma* (New York: Wang and Hill, 1984); James D. Roberts, *Liberation and Reconciliation: a Black Theology* (Philadelphia: Westminster Press, 1971).

   Among liberation theologies are included: Gustavo Gutierrez, *A Theology of Liberation* (Maryknoll, N.Y.: Orbis Books, 1973); Leonardo Boff, *Jesus Christ Liberator* (Maryknoll, N.Y.: Orbis Books, 1978); Jose Miguez Bonino, *Doing Theology in a Revolutionary Situation* (Philadelphia: Fortress Press, 1975); Juan Luis Segundo, *The Liberation of Theology* (Maryknoll, N.Y.: Orbis Books, 1976). From Africa, such works as Albert Nolan, *Jesus Before Christianity* (Maryknoll, N.Y.: Orbis Books, 1976); Allan A. Boesak, *Farewell to Innocence* (Maryknoll, N.Y.: Orbis Books, 1977). From Asia, *Minjung Theology* (Maryknoll, N.Y.: Orbis Book, 1983). All of these latter are written by men. Even collections published by the Ecumenical Association of Third World Theologians tend to offer largely male perspectives. Recently some collections by Third World women have appeared, such as Letty M. Russell, Kwok Pui-lan, Ada Maria Isasi-Diaz, and Katie Geneva Cannon, eds., *Inheriting Our Mothers' Gardens* (Philadelphia: The Westminster Press, 1988). This collection includes an extensive annotated bibliography. Virginia Fabella, M.M., and Mercy Amba Oduyoye, eds., *With Passion and Compassion* (Maryknoll, N.Y.: Orbis Books, 1988); Elsa Tamez, ed., *Through Her Eyes* (Maryknoll, N.Y.: Orbis Books, 1989).

13. Mary Daly, *Gyn/Ecology* (Boston: Beacon Press, 1978), *passim*.
14. Chung, Hyun Kyung, *Struggle to be the Sun Again*, 99.
15. Chung Hyun Kyung, *Struggle to be the Sun Again*, 93.
16. Jose Miguez Bonino, *Doing Theology in a Revolutionary Situation*, 99.
17. Chung Hyun Kyung, *Struggle to be the Sun Again*, 104.
18. This understanding is reflected in the title of a work on Buddhist-Christian dialogue by John B. Cobb, Jr., *Beyond Dialogue, Toward a Mutual Transformation of Christianity and Buddhism* (Philadelphia: Fortress Press, 1982).
19. Among the works reflecting such exchanges are found Kwesi A. Dickson, *Theology in Africa* (Maryknoll, N.Y.: Orbis Books, 1984); Gwinyai H. Muzorewa, *The Origins and Development of African Theology* (Maryknoll, N.Y.: Orbis Books, 1985); Kofi Appiah-Kubi & Sergio Torres, eds., *African Theology En Route* (Maryknoll, N.Y.: Orbis Books, 1979).
20. Cf. the series of articles in Rev. Sun Ai Park, ed., *In God's Image* (June 1989).
21. Aruna Gnanadason, "Women and Spirituality in Asia," *In God's Image* (December 1989), 18.
22. Some examples of Christian-Marxist encounters include: Paul Oestricher, *The Christian-Marxist Dialogue: an International Symposium* (New York: Macmillan, 1969); Peter Hebblewaite, *The Christian-Marxist Dialogue: Beginnings, Present Status and Beyond* (New York: Paulist Press, 1977); Roger Garaudy & Quentin Lauer, *A Christian-Communist Dialogue* (Garden City, N.Y.: Doubleday, 1968); Paul Maojzes, *Christian-Marxist Dialogue in Eastern Europe* (Minneapolis: Augsburg Publishing House, 1981).

Part Five

Chapter 9   The Poison Arrow, the Ringing Bell

1. Jose Miguez Bonino, *Doing Theology in a Revolutionary Situation*, 81.
2. Aarne Siirala, "Theology and the Unconscious," *Studies in Religion*, 6/6 (1976-77), 622.

3. Alves, *La Teología Como Juego*, chaps. 5, 6.
4. Chung Hyun Kyung, *Struggle to be the Sun Again*, 112.
5. Douglas John Hall, *The Future of the Church* (The United Church Publishing House, 1989), 58.
6. Reinhold Niebuhr, *The Nature and Destiny of Man* , vol. 2 (New York: Charles Scribner's Sons, 1949), 213-43.
7. Paul Tillich, *The Dynamics of Faith*, 1.
8. John Baillie, *Our Knowledge of God* (New York: Charles Scribner's Sons, 1959), 244.
9. Robert McAfee Brown, *Is Faith Obsolete?* (Philadelphia: The Westminster Press, 1974), 96.
10. John Baillie, *Our Knowledge of God*, 55.
11. Paul Tillich, *The Dynamics of Faith*, 20.

Story Collections
for further reading

Here are a few of the collections I found entertaining and illustrative.

Roy C. Amore and Larry D. Shinn. *Lustful Maidens and Ascetic Kings*. New York: Oxford University Press, 1981.

John Bailey, Kenneth McLeish, and David Spearman. *Gods and Men*. Oxford: Oxford University Press, 1981.

Martin Buber. *Tales of the Hasidim*. New York: Schoken Books, 1947.

Ella E. Clark. *Indian Legends of Canada*. Toronto: McClelland & Stewart, 1960.

———. *Indian Legends from the Northern Rockies*. Norman, Okla.: University of Oklahoma Press, 1966.

Cornelia Dimmitt and J.A.B. Buitenen, eds. *Classical Hindu Mythology*. Philadephia: Temple University Press, 1978.

Theodore H. Gaster. *The Oldest Stories in the World*. Boston: Beacon Press, 1952.

Louis Ginzberg. *The Legends of the Jews*. Philadelphia: Jewish Publication Society of America, 1901.

Douglas Hyde. *Legends of Saints and Sinners*. Dublin: Talbot Press, 1920.

A. L. Kroeber. *Yurok Myths*. Berkeley: University of California Press, 1976.

David Leeming. *Mythology: The Voyage of the Hero*, 2nd edition. New York: Harper & Row, 1981.

Idries Shah. *Tale of the Dervishes*. New York: E. P. Dutton, 1970.

————. *The Exploits of the Incomparable Mulla Nasrudin*. New York: E. P. Dutton, 1972.

Barbara C. Sproul. *Primal Myths: Creating the World*. New York: Harper & Row, 1979.

940182